A Season to Savor

RECIPES FOR MEMORABLE MOMENTS

A SEASON TO SAVOR
Recipes for Memorable Moments
Published by the Marist Parents' Club
Copyright © 2006
The Marist Parents' Club
Marist School
First Printing: 2006   15,000 copies
ISBN: 0-9626204-1-6
Library of Congress Number: 2006922377
Cover art: © Kathy Wochele
Photography: © Steve Cole

Additional copies of this book may be obtained by contacting
Marist Parents' Club
3790 Ashford-Dunwoody Road
Atlanta, Georgia 30319
770-457-7201
www.marist.com

Edited, Designed, and Manufactured by Favorite Recipes® Press
An imprint of

P.O. Box 305142
Nashville, Tennessee 37230
800-358-0560
Art Director: Steve Newman
Book Design: Starletta Polster
Project Editor: Anna Watson
Printed in China

ON THE COVER

The cover artwork is a stunning interpretation of the picturesque row of pin willow oaks that line the drive through the Marist Ashford-Dunwoody Campus. The painting was created by Marist parent and resident artist Kathy Wochele and carries special significance for thousands of families associated with the school. Throughout the year, the trees function as a living time line of student activities, often festooned with traditional blue and gold bows or bearing signs for upcoming events.

A Season to Savor

Dedication

A Season to Savor is dedicated to all

of the Marist mothers who have nurtured

the hearts, souls, and minds

of generations of Marist families.

Acknowledgments

ABOUT THE ARTIST . . .

A New Jersey native, cover artist Kathy Wochele skillfully captures the seasonal magic of the Marist campus in her impressionistic pastel landscape. The talented mother of five received her degree from the Tyler School of Art in Philadelphia before relocating to the Atlanta area. Early in her career, Kathy specialized in medical illustrations. Today, her work focuses on figure painting and portraits by commission. According to the artist, she enjoys painting her surroundings, skillfully capturing the light and pulling out all of the color and beauty she envisions.

ABOUT THE PHOTOGRAPHER . . .

Food photography throughout the book is the work of nationally acclaimed artist Steve Cole. A third-generation Atlanta native, Cole specializes in lifestyle photography for design firms and ad agencies around the world. His work has been featured in *Time* magazine, *Oprah*, and the *New York Times*. Four years ago, Cole and his wife, Janis Christie, opened their own studio in the Virginia Highlands section of Atlanta. Their talents are reflected in a diverse range of stock photography, including images focusing on sports, food, music, and the arts.

ABOUT THE FOOD STYLIST . . .

Freelance Atlanta food stylist Val Koonce has specialized in print and film media for local and national food companies for more than twenty years. A talented artist with degrees in nutrition, painting, and printmaking, Koonce has experience in display work for a full range of clients, from grocery chains and institutional food services to fine-dining restaurants and educational organizations.

SPECIAL THANKS . . .

Creation of *A Season to Savor* would not have been possible without the support of the Marist Parents' Club and the Marist School Alumni/Development Office. Special thanks also go to the staff of Infinitee Communications for sharing their graphic expertise; Marist historian Richard J. Reynolds III, '52, for his vast wisdom; and Marist parent Pam Zimmermann for procurement of the cover artwork. The contributions and culinary expertise of Trevor Kunk, from New York's Blue Hill Restaurant, were an invaluable asset to the project, as was the generosity of Kimberly Bitzer and Ellen Manning, owners of Kudzu Cottage in Alpharetta, Georgia, who graciously provided many of the accessories used in the photographs throughout the book. The support of these people, and countless members of the Marist School community working "behind the scenes," is truly appreciated.

Table of Contents

More than a century of history and tradition, filled with fascinating experiences, colorful characters, and an unwavering commitment to achievement in all arenas, is the key to the story of Marist School, an Atlanta institution since 1901. A treasured home to generations of Atlanta families, Marist has grown as quickly as the city that surrounds it, yet remains true to its founding ideals, specifically the pursuit of excellence in academic, religious, extracurricular, leadership, and service programs. Now in its second century, Marist continues to be a beloved center for learning and family life.

THE IVY STREET YEARS

The school first opened its doors to thirty-two young men as Marist College, an all-male military day school located in a three-story schoolhouse on Ivy Street in downtown Atlanta. It was founded by Father John E. Gunn, S.M., and owned and operated by the Society of Mary, a French religious order begun in 1836. Marist priests came to Atlanta at the turn of the century to serve the people of what is now Sacred Heart Parish, and they quickly identified the need for a Catholic school that would offer a quality education. At that time, Atlanta's public school system was in its infancy, with only two high schools in operation.

Soon, the growing city welcomed the Marist Cadets as willingly as Coca-Cola and cars, both of which were also making their debut. The Marist marching battalion participated in countless parades on historic Peachtree Street, beginning with the Confederate Memorial Day Parade in April 1903. Both in the classroom and on the marching ground, Marist was training the future leaders of the city.

Marist was also making great strides in educational circles. The award-winning student newspaper, the *Blue & Gold*, was started in 1914 and was the first high school newspaper written by students in the state. That same year, interscholastic football debuted at Marist and has remained a vital part of the school's tradition for the last century.

Under the watchful eye of the Reverend Philip Dagneau, S.M., Marist weathered the challenges of the new era, including the Great Depression, and continued to thrive. Although enrollment felt little impact, the greatest loss caused by the floundering economy was a summer camp established by Marist on Lake Rabun in the North Georgia mountains during the roaring twenties. The camp, situated on prime lakefront property, provided the perfect venue for the cadets to enjoy outdoor life, but the picturesque resort was sold as purse strings tightened.

World War II also had a profound effect on Marist, with many young men answering the call to duty, and military instruction moving into the classroom. Cadets were instructed in map reading, history, photography, and weaponry demonstration. Marist even began an aeronautics class to teach aviation mathematics and prepare the students for the "warfare of today." The 1940s were a significant era because of the expansion of athletics and the arts at Marist. The Marist athletes, appropriately called the Cadets, dominated football fields and basketball courts around the state. The same period witnessed the birth of the drama club, the "Maristagers," and the Glee Club. Enrollment mushroomed to more than 350 students, and soon school administrators were buying up surrounding property on Courtland Street in anticipation of an expansion.

THE ASHFORD-DUNWOODY YEARS

Fifteen years later, the expansion evolved into a full-scale relocation when Marist broke ground on a new fifty-six-acre campus in DeKalb County. Reflecting its role as a secondary school, Marist College officially became Marist School when it opened its doors on Ashford-Dunwoody Road in 1962.

The new location was just the beginning of several decades of growth and change at Marist. In 1976, young women were admitted, and the following year, military training was officially discontinued. With the arrival of plaid skirts and saddle shoes, the enrollment skyrocketed to more than eight hundred students. A new mascot, a live eagle named Mr. B, was welcomed to the campus, and the winning tradition of the Marist War Eagles was officially born.

Award-winning programs in all areas of education soon followed. The music and drama programs grew dramatically, evolving into a multidimensional extracurricular area for students with a marching band, jazz band, chorale, and theater department. Recently Marist was the recipient of the Ray Horne Award for excellence in debate, one-act play, and literary programs as the top high school program statewide. From the annual Sacred Concert to the blockbuster spring musicals, audiences pack the house at Marist to see productions.

Athletic programs have also kept pace with the growth and change at Marist. Today, about 80 percent of the student body participates in an interscholastic sport, and Marist has been the recipient of the AAAA Director's Cup for overall athletic program excellence every year since the award's inception. In 2005, Marist was named one of the top twenty-five high school athletic programs in the country by *Sports Illustrated* magazine. From the "long blue line" on the football field, to the state champion runners and tennis players, Marist students embrace the tradition of competition in each of the fourteen Varsity arenas.

Through these years of growth and change, service has remained at the heart of the Marist community. Student groups travel around the world on mission trips, and students and faculty can be found throughout the year working behind the scenes in countless Atlanta-based outreach programs to serve the poor. The school's Habitat for Humanity chapter was the first of its kind on any high school campus, and in 2003 Marist initiated the first all-women Habitat home build. Each year, Marist alumni, students, parents, and faculty work together on projects to serve those in need.

Academically, Marist has consistently maintained the standards of excellence established in the school's first days on Ivy Street. In recent years, Marist was recognized as a national Blue Ribbon School of Excellence by the U.S. Department of Education and was spotlighted by the College Board for the Advanced Placement programs that are offered in twenty-one subjects. Marist alumni are the business, civic, and community leaders of yesterday, today, and tomorrow.

Today, more than one thousand students gather every day on the sixty-seven-acre campus to continue the traditions started more than a century ago. The story of Marist is much richer, however, than the bricks and mortar described here. It is a drama played out by the families who remain committed to the school, the priests laboring tirelessly "under the name of Mary," and the teachers, coaches, and friends who see in today's generation of students tomorrow's generation of leaders.

The mission of Marist School is to form the whole person in the image of Christ through instruction grounded in religious values, the teachings of the Catholic Church, and the spirit of the Society of Mary. This mission is advanced through communal pursuit of excellence in academic, religious, extracurricular, leadership, and service programs.

Appetizers

From a simple salsa to

a tantalizing torte,

let the appetizer set the tone

for a special occasion.

Polenta Torte with Goat Cheese Sauce

Polenta
4 ounces pancetta or bacon, chopped
1 (10-ounce) package frozen chopped spinach, thawed and drained
4 cups water
1 teaspoon salt
1¹/2 cups yellow cornmeal
¹/2 cup (2 ounces) freshly grated Parmesan cheese
¹/2 cup diced drained roasted red bell pepper

Sauce
1 cup cream or heavy cream
2 tablespoons butter
4 ounces soft mild goat cheese, crumbled

Assembly
All-purpose flour for dusting
2 tablespoons olive oil

For the polenta, cook the pancetta in a large skillet until crisp; drain. Stir in the spinach. Bring the water and salt to a boil in a large saucepan. Whisk in the cornmeal gradually. Cook for 5 minutes, stirring constantly. Add the Parmesan cheese and mix well. Spoon 2 cups of the polenta into a buttered 9-inch pie plate and spread evenly. Top with the spinach mixture. Spread 1 cup of the polenta over the spinach and top with the roasted bell pepper. Spread the remaining polenta evenly over the top. Chill in the refrigerator, covered, for 3 hours or overnight until firm.

For the sauce, combine the cream and butter in a saucepan and bring to a boil. Whisk in the goat cheese until blended. Keep warm.

For the assembly, cut the chilled torte into wedges and dust lightly with flour. Heat the olive oil in a large nonstick skillet over medium-high heat. Add the wedges, a few at a time, and cook for about 8 minutes per side or until brown. Place the wedges on serving plates and spoon the warm sauce over the wedges.

Serves 6 to 8

Eggplant Roulade

Tomato Sauce
1 onion, chopped
2 tablespoons olive oil
1 small garlic clove, minced
2 pounds tomatoes, coarsely chopped
Pinch of sugar
Salt to taste

Eggplant Rolls
1 (1-pound) eggplant
1 cup (4 ounces) diced buffalo mozzarella cheese
3 1/2 ounces (about 1/2 cup) soft mild goat cheese, at room temperature
1/4 cup julienned fresh basil leaves
2 to 3 tablespoons olive oil
Fresh basil leaves for garnish

For the tomato sauce, cook the onion in the olive oil in a large heavy skillet over medium-low heat for 3 minutes, stirring occasionally. Add the garlic and cook until the onion is tender, stirring constantly. Add the tomatoes, sugar and salt. Cook over medium heat for 20 minutes, stirring occasionally. Purée the tomato mixture in a food mill or food processor. Place the puréed mixture in a saucepan and cook over medium-high heat for 5 to 10 minutes or until thickened to the desired consistency.

For the eggplant rolls, cut the eggplant lengthwise into 1/4-inch slices. Sprinkle with salt and drain in a colander for 30 minutes. Combine the mozzarella cheese, goat cheese and sliced basil in a bowl and mix well.

Preheat the broiler. Pat the eggplant slices dry and arrange in a single layer on an oiled broiler pan rack. Brush with half the olive oil. Broil 4 inches from the heat for 3 to 4 minutes or until golden brown. Turn the slices and brush with the remaining olive oil. Broil for 3 to 4 minutes or until golden brown. Place on a large platter to cool.

Spread a rounded teaspoon of the cheese mixture lengthwise down the center of each eggplant slice, leaving a 1-inch border along the sides. Starting at the narrow end, roll up jelly roll-fashion. Arrange seam-side down in an oiled shallow baking dish. Broil for 3 minutes or just until the cheese is melted and bubbly.

To serve, place the eggplant rolls on serving plates and spoon the tomato sauce over the rolls. Garnish with fresh basil.

Serves 4 to 6

Caramelized Onion Tartlets

1 tablespoon butter	1/2 cup cream or heavy cream
2 Vidalia onions, thinly sliced	1 tablespoon thyme leaves
Kosher salt or sea salt to taste	1 refrigerator pie crust
Freshly ground pepper to taste	4 ounces blue cheese, crumbled

Preheat the oven to 450 degrees. Melt the butter in a heavy skillet over medium-low heat. Add the onions and season with salt. Cook for about 25 minutes or until the onions are caramelized. Season with salt and pepper. Stir in the cream and thyme. Simmer until slightly thickened. Roll out the pie crust and cut out 4 rounds using a 3-inch round cutter. Crimp the edges and place the crusts on a baking parchment paper-lined baking sheet. Top each crust with the caramelized onions and the blue cheese. Bake for 10 to 12 minutes or until the cheese is melted and the crust is light brown. Serve warm or at room temperature.

Note: A silicone nonstick baking mat can be used instead of the parchment paper.

Serves 4

Warm Goat Cheese Toasts

1 baguette	1/2 cup walnuts or pecans,
2 cups (8 ounces) crumbled goat cheese	chopped and toasted
or shredded Swiss cheese or	1 1/2 teaspoons chopped fresh
Gruyère cheese	rosemary leaves
1 teaspoon kosher or sea salt	Freshly ground pepper to taste
1/4 cup honey	

Preheat the oven to 350 degrees. Cut the baguette into eighteen 1/4-inch slices. Top each slice with the cheese and sprinkle with salt. Arrange the slices on a large baking sheet. Bake for about 10 minutes or until golden brown. Drizzle with the honey. Sprinkle with the walnuts and rosemary. Return to the oven and bake for 2 minutes or until heated through. Season with pepper before serving.

Serves 6 to 8

Herbed Mushroom Onion Pizza

3 Vidalia onions
3 tablespoons butter
2 tablespoons plus 1 teaspoon
extra-virgin olive oil
1 teaspoon kosher salt
Freshly ground pepper to taste
1/4 cup (1/2 stick) butter
2 pounds assorted mushrooms,
cut into bite-size pieces
6 garlic cloves, minced

2 tablespoons minced shallots
2 cups dry white wine
1 tablespoon each, minced fresh
rosemary and thyme leaves
Kosher salt to taste
2 (8-ounce) balls fresh pizza dough or
prepared pizza crusts
Garlic oil
3 cups (12 ounces) shredded Gruyère or
fontina cheese or crumbled goat cheese

Place the oven rack in the lowest position. Place a large heavy baking sheet, bottom side up, or a pizza stone on the rack. Preheat the oven to 500 degrees. Cut the onions into halves and thinly slice. Sauté in 3 tablespoons butter and the olive oil in a large skillet over medium heat until golden brown. Season with 1 teaspoon salt and pepper. Melt 1/4 cup butter in another large skillet. Add the mushrooms, garlic and shallots and sauté for 4 minutes. Add the wine and simmer until the liquid is absorbed, stirring frequently. Stir in the rosemary, thyme and salt. Sprinkle another baking sheet with cornmeal. Roll out the pizza dough on a lightly floured surface into 8-inch rounds and place on the cornmeal-coated baking sheet. Brush with garlic oil. Top each evenly with the cheese, onions and mushroom mixture. Sprinkle with salt and pepper to taste. Slide the dough rounds onto the preheated baking sheet and bake for 6 minutes. Rotate the pizzas a half turn and bake 6 minutes longer or until the crust is brown. Remove the pizzas to a cutting board and let stand for 1 minute before slicing.

Makes 2 pizzas

Try these tasty combinations for this casual appetizer or main course:

Brush the crust with olive oil and add
- fresh tomatoes, chopped fresh basil, fresh mozzarella cheese, and minced garlic.
- sun-dried tomato pesto, fresh diced plum tomatoes, chopped fresh basil, crumbled goat cheese, and sliced prosciutto.
- sliced or chopped pears, crumbled gorgonzola cheese, and toasted walnuts.
- roasted red pepper, feta, sliced black olives, and chopped fresh oregano.

Try something new and grill your own pizza.
Roll the dough to desired size, and dust lightly with flour. Brush each side generously with olive oil and place on a preheated outdoor grill at medium heat. Cook for 1 to 3 minutes or until the underside is scored. Remove from the grill and top the toasted side with your favorite toppings. Return the pizza to the grill and continue cooking for 4 to 6 minutes or until desired doneness.

Spicy Chicken Satay

Peanut Sauce
1 cup coconut milk
1 tablespoon red curry paste
3/4 cup chunky peanut butter
1/2 cup chicken stock
1/4 cup packed brown sugar
2 tablespoons lime juice
1/2 teaspoon salt

Cucumber Relish
1/3 cup white vinegar
2 teaspoons brown sugar
1 teaspoon salt
1 large Japanese cucumber, peeled,
  halved and thinly sliced
2 shallots, thinly sliced
Fresh cilantro for garnish

Chicken Satay
1/2 cup coconut milk
1 tablespoon fish sauce
2 teaspoons red curry paste
1 teaspoon brown sugar
1 tablespoon chopped fresh cilantro
1/2 teaspoon turmeric
Salt and pepper to taste
1 pound boneless skinless chicken breasts

For the sauce, heat the coconut milk in a small saucepan until simmering. Whisk in the curry paste until dissolved. Whisk in the peanut butter, chicken stock and brown sugar. Reduce the heat and cook for 5 minutes, stirring constantly. Remove from the heat and stir in the lime juice and salt. Cool to room temperature.

For the relish, combine the vinegar, brown sugar and salt in a small saucepan and bring to a boil. Cook for 3 minutes. Remove from the heat and cool. Place the cucumbers and shallots in a large bowl. Pour the vinegar mixture over the cucumbers. Garnish with cilantro.

For the chicken, combine the coconut milk, fish sauce, curry paste, brown sugar, cilantro, turmeric, salt and pepper in a large bowl and mix well. Cut the chicken into long thin strips and add to the coconut milk mixture. Marinate, covered, in the refrigerator for up to 4 hours. Soak bamboo skewers in cold water. Preheat the grill. Remove the chicken strips from the marinade, discarding the marinade. Thread the chicken onto the skewers. Grill for 5 to 7 minutes or until the chicken is no longer pink. Serve with peanut sauce and cucumber relish.

Serves 4 to 6

Chicken Lettuce Wraps

Condiments
1/4 cup chopped red bell pepper
1/4 cup chopped green onions
Chow mein noodles (optional)
1/4 cup chopped fresh cilantro

Dipping Sauce
1/4 cup soy sauce
2 tablespoons water
1 tablespoon sugar

Chicken Wraps
1 tablespoon vegetable oil
1 boneless skinless chicken breast,
   finely chopped, or 1 pound
   ground chicken
1 or 2 garlic cloves, minced
1/2 teaspoon ground ginger
1/4 cup finely chopped or
   shredded carrots
1/4 cup finely chopped mushrooms
1/4 cup hoisin sauce
2 tablespoons oyster sauce
Dash of cayenne pepper
Salt and pepper to taste
12 large iceberg lettuce leaves

For the condiments, place the red bell pepper, green onions, chow mein noodles and cilantro in separate small serving bowls.

For the dipping sauce, combine the soy sauce, water and sugar in a bowl and mix well.

For the wraps, heat the oil in a skillet or saucepan over medium-high heat. Add the chicken and cook for 2 minutes, stirring constantly. Add the garlic and ginger and cook for 3 minutes, stirring constantly. Add the carrots and mushrooms and cook over medium heat for 3 to 5 minutes or until the vegetables are tender and the chicken is no longer pink. Stir in the hoisin sauce, oyster sauce and cayenne pepper. Season with salt and pepper. Remove from the heat.

To serve, place a large spoonful of the chicken mixture on a lettuce leaf and top with condiments. Roll up and serve with the dipping sauce.

Serves 6

Shrimp Won Tons with Pineapple Salsa

Salsa
1½ cups diced fresh pineapple
½ cup sugar
½ cup water
2 teaspoons chili garlic sauce
Juice of 1 lime

Won Tons
4 ounces cream cheese, softened
1 tablespoon minced fresh cilantro
2 teaspoons minced scallions
1 teaspoon minced fresh ginger
1 teaspoon sugar
1 teaspoon minced seeded jalapeño chile
Juice of ½ lime
1 cup (4 ounces) finely chopped cooked shrimp or crab meat
32 won ton wrappers
1 cup vegetable oil

For the salsa, combine the pineapple, sugar, water, chili sauce and lime juice in a small saucepan and bring to a boil over medium-high heat. Reduce the heat and simmer for 5 to 8 minutes or until thickened. Purée in a blender until smooth.

For the won tons, combine the cream cheese, cilantro, scallions, ginger, sugar, jalapeño and lime juice in a bowl and mix well. Fold in the shrimp. Arrange the won ton wrappers on a work surface. Place 1 teaspoon of the shrimp mixture in the center of each wrapper. Moisten the edges with water and fold into a triangle. Moisten the corners of the triangle and bring together, pinching to seal. Place on a baking parchment paper-lined baking sheet. Heat the oil to 350 degrees in a heavy saucepan or skillet over medium heat. Add the won tons, a few at a time, and fry for 2 to 3 minutes or until golden brown, turning once. Drain on paper towels. Serve with the salsa.

Makes 32 won tons

Dijon Vinaigrette Shrimp

3 pounds large shrimp, peeled and deveined
1 cup olive oil
1/2 cup Dijon mustard
1/2 cup tarragon vinegar
1/2 cup white wine vinegar

1/2 cup finely chopped parsley
1/2 cup chopped shallots
4 teaspoons red pepper flakes
1 tablespoon fresh lemon juice
2 teaspoons salt
Freshly ground pepper to taste

Cook the shrimp in a large pot of boiling salted water until the shrimp turn pink; drain. Place the shrimp in a large bowl. Combine the olive oil, Dijon mustard, tarragon vinegar, white wine vinegar, parsley, shallots, red pepper flakes, lemon juice, salt and pepper in a bowl and mix well. Pour over the warm shrimp and toss to coat the shrimp. Marinate, covered, in the refrigerator for at least 8 hours or overnight. Remove the shrimp from the vinaigrette and serve in a large lettuce-lined bowl.

Serves 8 to 10

SHRIMP WITH SNOW PEAS

Cook the shrimp as above and prepare the vinaigrette. Blanch 1 pound of snow peas in 2 quarts of boiling salted water in a large saucepan for 30 seconds. Drain; rinse under cold running water until cool. Pat dry. Split the snow peas in half lengthwise and wrap each around a shrimp. Secure with toothpicks. Place in a large bowl and pour the vinaigrette over the shrimp. Proceed as above.

Spicy Glazed Shrimp

Spicy Glaze
1 cup (2 sticks) butter
1/2 cup tomato paste
10 garlic cloves
2 tablespoons paprika
2 tablespoons salt
1 tablespoon sugar
1 1/2 teaspoons cayenne pepper

Shrimp
16 large shrimp, peeled and deveined, tails left on
Vegetable oil for frying
16 fresh basil leaves

For the glaze, place the butter, tomato paste, garlic, paprika, salt, sugar and cayenne pepper in a bowl and place over a saucepan of boiling water. Heat until the butter is melted, stirring occasionally. Pour into a blender or food processor and process until smooth. Chill in the refrigerator overnight.

For the shrimp, make a small cut on the back side of each shrimp near the tail and pull the tail through the cut. Heat a small amount of oil in a large skillet or sauté pan over high heat. Add half the shrimp. Cook for 2 to 3 minutes or until the shrimp turn pink, stirring constantly. Add 2 tablespoons of the glaze. Stir-fry the shrimp for 2 minutes longer or until glazed. Remove the shrimp from the pan. Wipe the pan and repeat the process with the remaining shrimp. Insert a basil leaf in the cut near the tail of each shrimp. Serve warm or at room temperature.

Serves 6 to 8

Prosciutto Palmiers

1 sheet frozen puff pastry, thawed
3 tablespoons honey mustard
4 ounces thinly sliced prosciutto

1 cup (4 ounces) freshly grated
Parmesan cheese
1 egg
1 tablespoon water

Preheat the oven to 375 degrees. Place the pastry sheet on a work surface and roll to an 11×18-inch rectangle. Spread the honey mustard over the pastry. Arrange the prosciutto evenly over the top, covering the pastry completely. Sprinkle the cheese over the prosciutto and press down lightly with a rolling pin. Starting at the long end, roll up the pastry, jelly roll-fashion, just to the center of the pastry. Roll up the other side in the same fashion, making 2 rolls that meet in the center. Cut the roll crosswise into 1/2-inch slices using a serrated knife. Place the slices on a baking parchment paper-lined baking sheet and press lightly to flatten. Chill in the refrigerator for 15 minutes. Beat the egg and water together in a small bowl. Brush the top of each palmier with the egg mixture. Bake for 10 to 12 minutes or until puffed and golden brown. Serve warm or at room temperature.

Makes 20 to 25 palmiers

Palmiers are an impressive appetizer with endless filling and presentation options. Use one of the interesting combinations listed here, or create your own flavorful medley. Remember to stay away from anything wet, which will result in soggy pastry. For variety:

- Spread the puff pastry with 1/3 cup of homemade or purchased pesto and sprinkle with Asiago cheese.
- For a French flair, spread a thin layer of country-style Dijon mustard, thinly sliced Black Forest ham, and a sprinkle of Gruyère cheese.
- A family-friendly filling would be a light spread of honey mustard, thinly sliced turkey, and a sprinkle of finely shredded mild Cheddar cheese.
- Sweeten it up with a spread of your favorite raspberry or strawberry preserves and a sprinkle of powdered sugar.
- Make a simple pastry cookie by generously sprinkling the puff pastry with cinnamon-sugar.
- All of the above must be sliced into 1/2-inch slices before baking.

Smoked Salmon Endive Spears

1/4 cup fresh lemon juice
1/4 cup finely chopped red onion
2 tablespoons chopped fresh dill weed
1 tablespoon Dijon mustard
1/2 cup olive oil

Salt and pepper to taste
24 Belgian endive leaves (3 large heads)
8 ounces thinly sliced smoked salmon,
  cut into 24 pieces
Sprigs of fresh dill weed

Whisk the lemon juice, onion, chopped dill weed and Dijon mustard in a small bowl until combined. Add the olive oil gradually, whisking constantly until blended. Season with salt and pepper. Arrange 3 endive leaves on each serving plate and top each with a piece of salmon. Drizzle with the dressing and top with the dill sprigs.

Note: The dressing and endive spears can be made 2 hours ahead. Chill, covered, in the refrigerator. Stir dressing before serving.

Serves 8

Salmon Pinwheels

8 ounces thinly sliced smoked salmon
4 ounces cream cheese, whipped
2 tablespoons finely chopped red onion
2 tablespoons capers, drained
  and chopped
2 tablespoons chopped fresh dill weed

1 1/2 teaspoons fresh lemon juice
Salt and pepper to taste
1 (1-pound) loaf cocktail pumpernickel
  bread, or crackers
Sprigs of fresh dill weed and capers for
  garnish

Arrange half the salmon in a single overlapping layer on a large sheet of plastic wrap to form a 7×9-inch rectangle. Combine the cream cheese, onion, 2 tablespoons capers, 2 tablespoons dill weed, lemon juice, salt and pepper in a bowl and mix well. Spread half the cream cheese mixture over the salmon to within 1/4 inch of the edges. Starting at the long end, roll up jelly roll-fashion, using the plastic wrap to help form the roll. Wrap the plastic wrap around the roll and twist the ends to seal. Repeat layering and rolling with the remaining salmon and cream cheese mixture. Freeze the salmon rolls for 1 hour.

Preheat the oven to 450 degrees. Cut a 2-inch round from each bread slice. Place the bread rounds on a baking sheet and bake for about 5 minutes or until light brown and crisp. Cool. Cut the salmon rolls into 1/4-inch slices using a serrated knife. Place the slices on the toasted bread and garnish with sprigs of dill weed and capers.

Makes 18 to 24 pinwheels

Eggplant Caponata

3 cups cubed peeled eggplant
1/3 cup diced green bell pepper
1 onion, sliced
4 ounces sliced mushrooms
2 garlic cloves, crushed
1/3 cup olive oil

1 (6-ounce) can tomato paste
1/4 cup water
2 tablespoons wine vinegar
1 1/2 tablespoons sugar
1/2 cup pimento-stuffed green
    olives, sliced

Combine the eggplant, bell pepper, onion, mushrooms, garlic and olive oil in a large saucepan or skillet over medium-low heat. Cook for 10 minutes, covered, stirring occasionally. Add the tomato paste, water, vinegar, sugar and olives and mix well. Simmer, covered, for 30 minutes, stirring occasionally. Chill in the refrigerator. Serve with crackers, toasted Italian bread slices or pita chips.

Makes about 3 cups

Olive Tapenade

2 garlic cloves
1 shallot
1/2 cup fresh basil leaves
1/4 cup fresh parsley

1/2 cup black olives, drained and pitted
1/2 cup green olives, drained and pitted
Balsamic vinegar to taste
Olive oil

Place the garlic and shallot in a food processor and pulse to chop. Add the basil and parsley and process just until chopped. Add the olives and chop by pulsing 5 times. Add vinegar. Add the oil in a fine stream and process to the consistency of a chopped relish. Serve with French bread rounds and blue cheese or Brie cheese.

Serves 8

Basil Blue Cheese Torte

1 cup fresh basil leaves
1 cup chopped fresh spinach
1 teaspoon minced garlic
$1/4$ cup olive oil
1 cup (4 ounces) grated Parmesan cheese
Salt and pepper to taste
8 ounces cream cheese, softened
4 ounces blue cheese or goat cheese, crumbled
$1/4$ cup finely chopped walnuts or pine nuts
$1/4$ cup thinly sliced well-drained oil-pack sun-dried tomatoes

Line a 3-cup bowl with plastic wrap, extending the plastic wrap 4 inches over the edge. Combine the basil, spinach and garlic in a food processor and process until finely chopped. Add the olive oil in a fine stream, processing constantly. Add the Parmesan cheese and process until combined. Season with salt and pepper. Combine the cream cheese and blue cheese in a mixing bowl and beat well.

Spoon one-third of the cream cheese mixture into the prepared bowl and spread evenly. Spread half the basil mixture over the cheese. Sprinkle with half the walnuts and half the sun-dried tomatoes. Spoon half the remaining cream cheese mixture over the top and spread evenly. Repeat the layering process with the remaining ingredients, ending with the cream cheese mixture.

Fold the plastic wrap over the mixture to cover completely and press down gently. Chill in the refrigerator overnight. Unfold the plastic wrap from the top of the torte and invert the bowl onto a serving plate. Remove the bowl and plastic wrap. Let stand for 30 minutes at room temperature before serving. Serve with crackers.

Serves 8 to 10

Smoked Trout Spread

6 to 8 ounces smoked trout, skinned and flaked
8 to 12 ounces whipped cream cheese
Juice of 1/2 lemon, or to taste
4 or 5 drops of hot pepper sauce, or to taste
1 to 2 tablespoons rinsed drained capers
2 or 3 scallions, finely chopped

Combine the trout, cream cheese, lemon juice, hot sauce, capers and scallions in a medium bowl and stir gently. Spoon into a serving bowl. Serve with lavash, pretzels, crackers or bagel chips.

Note: For a creamier spread, add sour cream to reach the desired consistency.
Smoked salmon or smoked whitefish can be substituted for the trout.

Serves 20 to 30

Blue Cheese Parsley Dip

2 bunches curly-leaf parsley, stems removed
1 small red onion, finely chopped
8 ounces crumbled blue cheese
Balsamic vinaigrette or cherry mustard balsamic vinaigrette

Finely chop the parsley. Layer half the parsley on a serving platter. Top with half the onion and half the blue cheese. Repeat the layers. Make slits in the layers with a knife. Pour the vinaigrette over the layers, allowing the vinaigrette to soak in. Chill in the refrigerator for 1 hour or until firm. Serve with thin wheat crackers.

Note: A layer of diced fresh tomatoes can be sprinkled on top of the
dip for a lovely summer accent.

Serves 10 to 12

Red Pepper Dip

1 or 2 red bell peppers, roasted, peeled,
seeded and chopped, or 1 (8-ounce) jar
roasted peppers, drained
1 cup mayonnaise
1 tablespoon Dijon mustard

1 garlic clove, minced
1 teaspoon grated lemon zest
1 tablespoon lemon juice
3 drops of hot pepper sauce

Combine the bell peppers, mayonnaise, Dijon mustard, garlic, lemon zest, lemon juice and hot sauce in a food processor and process until blended. Pour into a serving bowl. Serve with pita chips or assorted fresh vegetables such as asparagus, snow peas, sugar snap peas and blanched green beans.

Note: Ground chipotle chile or fresh cilantro can be added, if desired. For a pretty presentation, serve the dip in yellow or green bell pepper halves.

Makes 1 1/2 cups

Shrimp Salsa

This is a great appetizer for a crowd!

2 (14-ounce) cans diced peeled
tomatoes, drained
2 avocados, peeled and finely chopped
1 small Vidalia onion, finely chopped
1 large bunch fresh cilantro,
finely chopped
1/4 cup ketchup

3 tablespoons fresh lemon juice
3 tablespoons fresh orange juice
4 dashes of Tabasco sauce
1/2 teaspoon crushed red pepper flakes
8 ounces cooked shrimp, peeled, deveined
and coarsely chopped

Combine the tomatoes, avocados, onion, cilantro, ketchup, lemon juice, orange juice, Tabasco sauce and red pepper flakes in a large bowl and mix well. Chill, covered, in the refrigerator for 1 hour or longer. Stir in the shrimp just before serving. Pour into a serving bowl. Serve with tortilla chips.

Serves 10

Black-Eyed Pea Salsa

1 (14-ounce) can black-eyed peas,
drained and rinsed
2 tomatoes, chopped
1 bunch green onions, sliced
1/3 cup chopped fresh cilantro
1/4 cup olive oil
3 tablespoons fresh lime juice

1 tablespoon chopped jalapeño chile
2 garlic cloves, minced
1/2 teaspoon ground cumin
1/2 teaspoon pepper
1/4 teaspoon salt
1 avocado, chopped

Combine the black-eyed peas, tomatoes, green onions, cilantro, olive oil, lime juice, jalapeño, garlic, cumin, pepper and salt in a large bowl and mix well. Chill, covered, in the refrigerator for at least 4 hours or overnight. Stir in the avocado just before serving. Pour into a serving bowl. Serve with tortilla chips, corn chips or red and green bell pepper strips.

Note: This salsa can be made up to three days ahead.

Makes 2 1/2 cups

SALSA IS ONE OF THE MOST VERSATILE DISHES CHEFS OF all levels can master with ease, ideal for casual entertaining or events on the go like picnics and tailgates. At Marist, families rely on crowd-pleasing recipes like Shrimp Salsa when friends of all ages gather for sporting event tailgates, Peer Leader parties, and weekend retreats. Served with chips or a colorful blend of fresh vegetables, salsa made with fresh cilantro has become the perfect tangy temptation. After the party, leftover salsa can be refrigerated and used to give a spicy boost to eggs, sandwiches, and even grilled fish or chicken.

Salads

Sensational salads that are fresh,

crisp, and flavorful serve as delicious

beginnings or main courses.

Mexican Salad

Cilantro Lime Dressing
1 cup olive oil
1/2 cup fresh lime juice
1 cup fresh cilantro leaves
5 scallions
Salt and pepper to taste

Salad
3 ears of corn, roasted
2 tablespoons olive oil
2 heads red leaf lettuce, torn into bite-size pieces
1/2 red bell pepper, chopped
1/2 yellow bell pepper, chopped
1 avocado, sliced
1/2 to 3/4 cup chopped pistachios
1 cup (4 ounces) shredded Cheddar cheese
1 1/2 cups crushed blue corn chips

For the dressing, combine the olive oil, lime juice, cilantro, scallions, salt and pepper in a blender and process until smooth.

For the salad, cut the corn from the cobs and sauté in the olive oil in a skillet for 4 to 5 minutes; cool. Combine the lettuce, sautéed corn, bell peppers, avocado, pistachios and cheese in a large serving bowl. Add the dressing and toss gently. Top with the crushed corn chips and serve immediately.

Serves 8

Winter Beet, Cucumber and Goat Cheese Salad

Beets have always had a bad rap. They tend to taste "earthy" and the thought
of beet juice will make the average Joe cringe. This recipe eliminates
that bad reputation beets have inherited. In this unique salad, the beets are
complemented by the fresh crispness of the cucumber, the smooth sharpness of
the goat cheese, and the sweetness of the honey.

Dressing	Salad
1/4 cup rice wine vinegar or champagne vinegar	1 large red beet
1 tablespoon orange juice	1 large golden beet
1 teaspoon honey	2 European cucumbers, peeled, seeded and diced
1/2 teaspoon dry mustard	1 small bunch arugula, stems removed, rinsed well and dried
1 small bunch chives, finely chopped	4 ounces soft mild goat cheese, crumbled
1/2 cup plus 2 tablespoons vegetable oil	
Salt and pepper to taste	

For the dressing, whisk together the vinegar, orange juice, honey, dry mustard and chives in a bowl until combined. Add the oil gradually, whisking constantly until combined. Season with salt and pepper.

For the salad, place the beets in salted water in a saucepan. Boil over medium-high heat for 30 minutes or until the beets are fork tender. Drain and cool. Peel and dice the beets. Combine the beets and the dressing in a medium serving bowl. Add the cucumbers and arugula and stir gently. Sprinkle with the goat cheese and serve.

Serves 4

A FAMILY TRADITION OF CULINARY BRILLIANCE AND A diverse European education is the foundation that Chef Patrick Albrecht, Marist class of 1992, brings to the table when preparing specialty dishes like this warm winter salad. Son of nationally known Atlanta Chef Paul Albrecht, the founder of Pano's & Paul's, Patrick is a 1999 graduate of the Culinary Institute in Miesbach, Germany. He worked in several of the award-winning Buckhead Life Group restaurants and his father's highly acclaimed eatery in Carillon Beach, Florida, before being appointed to his first position as Executive Chef in a major Florida hotel and resort. In 2003, Albrecht returned to his Atlanta roots to become partners with Chef William Neal in his highly acclaimed catering company, and today he delights customers all over the city with superior cuisine and breathtaking presentation for special events of all kinds.

Chilled Greens with Warm Brie Dressing

Dressing
1/2 cup olive oil
4 teaspoons minced shallots
2 teaspoons minced garlic
1/2 cup sherry vinegar
2 tablespoons fresh lemon juice
4 teaspoons Dijon mustard
10 ounces ripe Brie cheese, softened and
cut into cubes
Freshly ground pepper

Croutons
1 garlic clove, minced
1/4 cup olive oil
3 cups French bread cubes

Salad
1 (10-ounce) package mixed salad greens, or
2 large heads romaine, torn into
bite-size pieces and chilled
1 Granny Smith apple or pear, sliced

For the dressing, warm the olive oil in a heavy skillet over low heat for 10 minutes. Add the shallots and garlic and cook for 5 minutes until translucent, stirring occasionally. Stir in the vinegar, lemon juice and Dijon mustard until combined. Add the cheese and heat until melted and smooth, stirring constantly. Season with pepper.

For the croutons, sauté the garlic in the olive oil in a skillet over medium heat. Add the bread cubes and cook until light brown on all sides, stirring constantly.

For the salad, arrange the greens and apple on serving plates. Drizzle with the dressing and top with the croutons.

Serves 8

Crunchy Romaine Toss

Dressing
1 cup vegetable oil
1 cup sugar
$1/2$ cup red wine vinegar
1 tablespoon soy sauce
Salt and pepper to taste

Salad
$1/4$ cup ($1/2$ stick) butter
1 cup chopped pecans
1 (3-ounce) package ramen noodles, crushed (do not use flavor packet)
2 bunches romaine, finely chopped
1 head broccoli, separated into small florets
1 bunch green onions, sliced

For the dressing, combine the oil, sugar, vinegar, soy sauce, salt and pepper in a blender or a jar with a tight-fitting lid and process or shake until blended.

For the salad, melt the butter in a large skillet over medium heat. Add the pecans and noodles and sauté until golden brown; cool. Combine the romaine, broccoli, green onions and pecan mixture in a large serving bowl. Pour the desired amount of dressing over the salad and toss.

Serves 10

Baby Blue Salad

Sweet and Spicy Pecans
1/4 cup sugar
1 cup warm water
1 cup pecan halves
2 tablespoons sugar
1 tablespoon chili powder
1/8 teaspoon cayenne pepper

Balsamic Vinaigrette
1/2 cup balsamic vinegar
3 tablespoons coarse Dijon mustard
3 tablespoons honey
2 garlic cloves, minced
2 small shallots, minced
1/4 teaspoon salt
1/4 teaspoon pepper
1 cup olive oil

Salad
12 ounces mixed salad greens
4 ounces blue cheese, crumbled
2 oranges, peeled and thinly sliced
1 pint strawberries, quartered

For the pecans, combine 1/4 cup sugar and the water in a bowl, stirring until the sugar dissolves. Add the pecans and let stand for 10 minutes; drain, discarding the liquid. Preheat the oven to 350 degrees. Combine 2 tablespoons sugar, the chili powder and cayenne pepper in a medium bowl. Add the pecans, tossing to coat. Spread the pecans on a lightly greased or foil-lined baking sheet. Bake for 10 minutes or until golden brown, stirring once; cool.

For the vinaigrette, whisk together the vinegar, Dijon mustard, honey, garlic, shallots, salt and pepper in a medium bowl until combined. Add the olive oil gradually, whisking constantly until blended.

For the salad, toss the greens and the blue cheese with the vinaigrette in a large bowl. Divide among 6 individual serving plates. Arrange the orange slices over the greens and top with the strawberries and the pecans.

Serves 6

Mixed Green Salad with Roquefort Vinaigrette

8 cups mixed baby greens
8 ounces plum tomatoes, seeded
   and diced
4 chopped green onions
1/4 cup dried cranberries or
   dried currants
1/2 cup toasted chopped pecans

1/2 cup plus 1 tablespoon olive oil
3 tablespoons raspberry vinegar or
   red wine vinegar
Salt and pepper to taste
1/2 cup (2 ounces) crumbled
   Roquefort cheese

Combine the baby greens, tomatoes, green onions, dried cranberries and pecans in a large salad bowl and mix well. Whisk the olive oil and the raspberry vinegar in a small bowl and season with salt and pepper. Stir in the Roquefort cheese and mix well. Toss the salad with the vinaigrette and serve.

Serves 6

Cheese, fruits, and nuts are perfect ways to dress up any combination of fresh greens. Experiment with some of the following:

- Wake up fruit with an orange vinaigrette. Combine 3 1/2 tablespoons olive oil, 2 tablespoons white wine vinegar, 3 tablespoons orange juice, and 1 tablespoon grated orange zest.
- Top with crisp, crumbled bacon or pancetta.
- Replace the oranges with sliced fresh pears or tart apples.
- Sprinkle with dried cherries.
- Use feta cheese instead of blue cheese.
- Toss in thinly sliced Vidalia onions or red onions.
- Experiment with flavored vinegar.
- Add pine nuts for a flavorful crunch.

When serving a hearty entrée, keep it simple and delicious by mixing crisp mixed greens with freshly prepared Balsamic Vinaigrette (page 32).

Fig and Stilton Salad

Vinaigrette and Fig Dressing
3/4 cup ruby port
1/4 cup dry red wine
1/4 cup vegetable oil
3 tablespoons balsamic vinegar
2 tablespoons hazelnut oil or walnut oil
1 tablespoon sugar
1 tablespoon red wine vinegar
1 1/2 teaspoons Worcestershire sauce
1 1/2 teaspoons light molasses
1/4 teaspoon onion powder
1 (9-ounce) package dried Black Mission
figs, stemmed and cut in half lengthwise (about 1 3/4 cups)
Salt and pepper to taste

Salad
5 ounces mixed baby greens
4 ounces Stilton cheese, crumbled

For the dressing, whisk together the port, red wine, vegetable oil, balsamic vinegar, hazelnut oil, sugar, red wine vinegar, Worcestershire sauce, molasses and onion powder in a medium bowl until blended. The vinaigrette can be made up to this point 3 days ahead. Store, covered, in the refrigerator. Combine the vinaigrette and the figs in a heavy nonstick skillet. Simmer over medium-high heat for about 8 minutes or until the mixture is slightly syrupy, stirring occasionally. Season with salt and pepper.

For the salad, divide the greens among 6 individual serving plates. Sprinkle with the cheese. Spoon the fig dressing over the salads.

Serves 6

San Francisco Salad

Dressing
1/2 cup red wine vinegar or
   balsamic vinegar
1/2 cup vegetable oil or olive oil
1 cup finely chopped parsley
1/2 cup finely chopped red onion
2 tablespoons sugar
1 garlic clove, minced
1 teaspoon oregano
1/4 teaspoon salt
1/4 teaspoon pepper

Peppered Walnuts
3 tablespoons butter
1 cup walnut halves
1/2 cup sugar
1 tablespoon pepper

Salad
1 (10-ounce) package mixed salad
   greens
3/4 cup dried cranberries
8 ounces feta cheese, crumbled

For the dressing, combine the vinegar, oil, parsley, onion, sugar, garlic, oregano, salt and pepper in a blender and process until smooth. The dressing can be made several days in advance. Store, covered, in the refrigerator.

For the walnuts, melt the butter in a small skillet and add the walnuts. Sauté until light brown. Stir together the sugar and pepper in a bowl. Drain the walnuts and add to the sugar mixture, tossing to coat. Shake off any excess sugar mixture with a slotted spoon.

For the salad, combine the greens, dried cranberries, cheese and walnuts in a large bowl and mix well. Add the dressing and toss just before serving.

Serves 8

Poppy Seed Summer Salad

Poppy Seed Dressing
3/4 cup canola oil
1/2 cup honey
1 tablespoon dry mustard
1 tablespoon poppy seeds
1 tablespoon apple cider vinegar
1 teaspoon salt

Salad
2 (10-ounce) packages baby
    spinach leaves
1 (4-ounce) package dried banana chips
1 (11-ounce) can mandarin oranges,
    drained
1/2 pint raspberries
1/2 pint blackberries or blueberries
8 ounces strawberries, sliced
1 small package slivered almonds
1/2 red onion, sliced
1/2 cup walnut pieces (optional)

For the dressing, combine the canola oil, honey, dry mustard, poppy seeds, vinegar and salt in a small saucepan and warm over low heat until combined, stirring occasionally. You may also combine the ingredients in a microwave-safe container and microwave for 15 seconds; stir.

For the salad, combine the spinach, dried banana chips, oranges, berries, almonds, onion and walnuts in a large serving bowl. Whisk the dressing and pour over the salad, tossing to coat. Serve immediately.

Serves 8 to 10

Spinach Salad with Mango Chutney Dressing

Dressing
1/4 cup balsamic vinegar
3 to 4 tablespoons mango chutney
2 tablespoons Dijon mustard
1 or 2 garlic cloves, crushed
3 tablespoons sugar
1/2 cup vegetable oil

Salad
1 (10-ounce) package baby
    spinach leaves
2 tart apples, diced
4 ounces sliced mushrooms
1/2 red onion, sliced
1/2 cup walnut pieces

For the dressing, combine the vinegar, chutney, Dijon mustard, garlic and sugar in a food processor and process until smooth. Add the oil in a steady stream, processing constantly until blended.

For the salad, combine the spinach, apples, mushrooms, onion and walnuts in a large serving bowl. Add the dressing and toss to coat. Serve immediately.

Serves 6 to 8

Watercress and Watermelon Salad

2 tablespoons rice vinegar
1 1/2 tablespoons vegetable oil
2 teaspoons minced peeled
fresh ginger
1 1/2 teaspoons grated lime zest
1 garlic clove, minced
Salt and pepper to taste

2 cups diced peeled seedless watermelon
1 large bunch watercress, stems removed
(about 2 cups packed)
1 cup diced seeded peeled cucumber
4 green onions, sliced
1/4 cup chopped fresh cilantro
2 tablespoons chopped fresh mint leaves

Whisk together the vinegar, oil, ginger, lime zest and garlic in a large bowl until blended. Season with salt and pepper. Add the watermelon, watercress, cucumber, green onions, cilantro and mint and toss to coat. Divide the salad among 4 individual serving plates.

Serves 4

Orange Cucumber Relish

2 tablespoons rice vinegar
2 tablespoons sugar
1 tablespoon minced pickled ginger
1/2 teaspoon kosher salt
1/4 teaspoon red pepper flakes (optional)
2 cups fresh orange sections

1 cup thinly sliced English cucumber
1/2 cup fresh bean sprouts
1/4 cup torn fresh cilantro leaves
1/4 cup thinly sliced scallions
(green parts only)
1 tablespoon minced fresh mint leaves

Whisk together the vinegar, sugar, ginger, salt and red pepper flakes in a large bowl until the sugar dissolves. Add the oranges, cucumber, bean sprouts, cilantro, scallions and mint and toss to coat. Serve immediately.

Makes 4 cups

Chilled Asparagus Salad

1 pound asparagus, cut into
2-inch pieces
1 red bell pepper, cut into strips
1/3 cup vegetable oil
1/3 cup red wine vinegar or
garlic vinegar
3 green onions, chopped

3 garlic cloves, minced
1/4 teaspoon basil
1/4 teaspoon sugar
8 ounces sliced salami, cut into strips
1/2 cup (2 ounces) crumbled feta cheese
Lettuce leaves

Microwave the asparagus in a small amount of water in a microwave-safe dish on High for 1 to 2 minutes or until tender-crisp. Rinse under cold running water until cool; drain. Place the asparagus and bell pepper in a large bowl. Whisk together the oil, vinegar, green onions, garlic, basil and sugar in a small bowl until combined. Pour over the asparagus mixture and mix well. Marinate, covered, in the refrigerator for 2 to 3 hours or overnight. Add the salami and cheese and toss. Line a platter with the lettuce and top with the salad.

Serves 4 to 6

Greek Salad

12 ounces tomatoes, seeded and diced
(about 2 cups)
2 cups diced cucumber
1 cup diced red bell pepper
1/4 cup pitted kalamata olives
1/4 cup diced red onion
3 tablespoons chopped fresh parsley

3 tablespoons olive oil
1 1/2 tablespoons red wine vinegar
1/2 teaspoon oregano
1/4 cup to 1/2 cup (1 to 2 ounces)
crumbled feta cheese
Salt and pepper to taste

Combine the tomatoes, cucumber, bell pepper, olives, onion, parsley, olive oil, vinegar and oregano in a large bowl and mix gently. Stir in the cheese. Season with salt and pepper. The salad can be made several hours ahead. Let stand at room temperature before serving.

Note: For a lighter version, reduce the olive oil to 1 tablespoon.

Serves 4 to 6

Creamy Tomato and Cucumber Salad

1 teaspoon cumin seeds
1 English cucumber, peeled,
  seeded and cubed
1 tablespoon chopped onion

1 1/2 teaspoons kosher salt
2 tomatoes, cubed
3 tablespoons chopped fresh cilantro
3/4 cup plain yogurt

Toast the cumin seeds in a small nonstick skillet over medium heat for 30 seconds. Combine the cucumber, onion and salt in a bowl and let stand at room temperature for 10 minutes. Place in a strainer and press with a spoon to remove the excess liquid. Combine the cucumber mixture, tomatoes and cilantro in a bowl. Combine the yogurt and cumin seeds in a small bowl and mix well. Stir into the cucumber mixture. Chill, covered, in the refrigerator for 1 hour. Stir before serving.

Serves 2 to 4

Tomato Feta Salad

2 pints cherry tomatoes,
  halved and seeded
1 (4-ounce) can pitted black olives,
  drained and chopped
1/2 cup fresh basil leaves, chopped,
  or to taste

1/2 cup diced red onion, or to taste
1 cup (4 ounces) crumbled feta cheese
Salt and pepper to taste
2 tablespoons olive oil

Combine the tomatoes, olives, basil, onion and cheese in a bowl. Season with salt and pepper. Drizzle with the olive oil and stir gently.

Serves 4

Jalapeño Basil Slaw

Slaw

1/2 head green cabbage, thinly sliced
1/2 head red cabbage, thinly sliced
1 (6- to 8-ounce) package shredded
   carrots, or 5 carrots, shredded
1 small red onion or sweet white
   onion, thinly sliced
2 jalapeño chiles, seeded and
   finely chopped
1 cup packed fresh cilantro leaves
   (1 bunch)

Dressing

1 cup packed fresh basil leaves,
   stems removed
1 shallot, chopped
2 garlic cloves, coarsely chopped
1 cup canola oil
2 tablespoons honey, or to taste
1/2 cup champagne vinegar or
   rice vinegar
1 teaspoon kosher salt
1/2 teaspoon pepper

For the slaw, combine the cabbage, carrots, onion, jalapeños and cilantro in a large bowl and mix well. Chill, covered, in the refrigerator until ready to serve.

For the dressing, place the basil, shallot, garlic and canola oil in a blender and process until smooth. Add the honey, vinegar, salt and pepper and process until combined. Pour the dressing over the slaw 5 minutes before serving and toss.

Note: The beautiful green color of the dressing doesn't hold, so make the dressing just before serving.

Serves 8 to 10

Winter Slaw

Dressing

1/2 cup (2 ounces) crumbled
   blue cheese
1/2 cup red wine vinegar
1 tablespoon Dijon mustard
1 large garlic clove, minced
1/2 cup olive oil

Slaw

1 head cabbage, shredded
8 ounces sliced ham, cut into thin strips
8 ounces sliced Gruyére cheese, cut into
   thin strips
6 tablespoons chopped fresh parsley
Salt and pepper to taste

For the dressing, combine the blue cheese, vinegar, Dijon mustard and garlic in a food processor and process until smooth. Add the olive oil in a steady stream, processing constantly until blended.

For the slaw, combine the cabbage, ham, Gruyére cheese and parsley in a large bowl. Add the dressing and mix well. Season with salt and pepper. Chill, covered, in the refrigerator for 6 to 8 hours before serving.

Serves 8

Orzo and Black Bean Salad

Dressing
2/3 cup olive oil
3 tablespoons lime juice
1¹/2 tablespoons white wine vinegar
2 garlic cloves, crushed
1¹/2 teaspoons ground cumin
¹/2 teaspoon salt
Dash of Tabasco sauce, or to taste

Salad
8 ounces orzo, cooked, rinsed
  and drained
1 red bell pepper, chopped
1 yellow bell pepper, chopped
1 sweet onion, diced
2 (15-ounce) cans black beans, drained
  and rinsed
1 pint grape tomatoes, cut into halves
8 ounces basil and tomato feta cheese,
  crumbled
¹/3 cup chopped fresh cilantro
Lettuce leaves

For the dressing, whisk together the olive oil, lime juice, vinegar, garlic, cumin, salt and Tabasco sauce in a small bowl until blended.

For the salad, combine the orzo, bell peppers, onion, beans, tomatoes, cheese and cilantro in a large bowl. Add the dressing and mix well. Chill, covered, in the refrigerator for several hours before serving. Line a platter with lettuce and top with the salad.

Serves 12 to 15

Spinach Orzo Salad with Pine Nuts

8 ounces orzo, cooked, rinsed,
  drained and cooled
3 tablespoons olive oil
Grated zest and juice of
  1 lemon

1 (10-ounce) package baby spinach
  leaves, julienned
1 cup (4 ounces) (or more) crumbled
  feta cheese
¹/2 cup (or more) pine nuts, toasted

Combine the orzo, olive oil, lemon zest, lemon juice, spinach and cheese in a large bowl and mix well. Spoon into a serving bowl. Top with the pine nuts just before serving.

Serves 8 to 10

Blackened Steak Salad

Dressing
1/4 cup olive oil
2 tablespoons balsamic vinegar
1 teaspoon Dijon mustard
Salt and pepper to taste
Greek seasoning to taste
1/2 red bell pepper, thinly sliced
1/2 cup thinly sliced red onion

Salad
3 to 4 tablespoons Cajun seasoning or
blackening seasoning
2 (5- to 6-ounce) beef tenderloin steaks, about 1/2-inch thick
3 tablespoons butter, melted
6 cups packed mixed baby greens
3 ounces blue cheese, crumbled (about 6 tablespoons)
1 large tomato, chopped

For the dressing, whisk together the olive oil, vinegar and Dijon mustard in a large bowl until blended. Season with salt, pepper and Greek seasoning. Add the bell pepper and onion and mix well. Let stand at room temperature for 2 hours or longer.

For the salad, spread the Cajun seasoning on a plate. Coat the steaks in the seasoning on both sides. Dip the steaks in the butter, coating both sides. Heat a large heavy skillet over high heat until very hot. Add the steaks and cook for about 2 minutes per side for medium-rare or to the desired degree of doneness. You may also grill the steaks over medium direct heat to desired doneness. Remove the steaks to a cutting board and let stand for 2 minutes. Cut the steaks diagonally into thin slices. Add the greens to the dressing mixture and toss. Divide the greens between 2 individual serving plates. Top with the steak slices. Sprinkle with the cheese and tomato.

*Note: Other vegetables, such as grilled asparagus, can be added to the salad.
Shrimp or chicken can be substituted for the steaks.*

Serves 2

Spring Salad with Shallot Vinaigrette

Salad
1¹/2 pounds small red-skin potatoes,
cut into wedges
1¹/2 pounds carrots, peeled and
halved lengthwise
1¹/2 pounds asparagus, trimmed and
cut into 2-inch pieces
6 ounces sugar snap peas, trimmed
18 ounces low-fat cooked ham or
smoked turkey, julienned

Vinaigrette
¹/2 cup chopped shallots
¹/3 cup seasoned rice vinegar
1¹/2 teaspoons Dijon mustard
1¹/2 tablespoons olive oil
Salt and pepper to taste
Spinach leaves

For the salad, cook the potatoes and carrots in a large saucepan of boiling salted water for 7 minutes or until almost tender. Add the asparagus and sugar snap peas and cook for 3 minutes longer or until the vegetables are tender-crisp; drain. Rinse under cold running water until cool. Drain and place in a large bowl. The vegetables can be prepared 1 day ahead. Store, covered, in the refrigerator. Add the ham to the vegetable mixture when ready to serve.

For the vinaigrette, whisk together the shallots, vinegar and Dijon mustard in a small bowl until blended. Whisk in the olive oil gradually. Season with salt and pepper.

To serve, add the vinaigrette to the vegetable mixture and toss to coat. Season with additional salt and pepper, if desired. Line a platter with spinach leaves and spoon the salad on top.

Serves 8

Bistro Chicken Salad with Feta

4 boneless skinless chicken breasts
6 cups cooked penne or rotini pasta
2 cups quartered cherry tomatoes
8 ounces basil and tomato
feta cheese, crumbled
1 cup creamy Caesar salad dressing
1/2 cup lightly packed fresh basil leaves, julienned
1/2 cup chopped red onion
1/2 cup oil-pack sun-dried tomatoes,
drained and chopped

Sauté or poach the chicken until no longer pink. Cool and cut into bite-size pieces. Combine the chicken, pasta, cherry tomatoes, cheese, salad dressing, basil, onion and sun-dried tomatoes in a large bowl and mix well. Serve warm or chilled.

Serves 6 to 8

Creamy Caesar Salad Dressing

2 egg yolks (pasteurized or
coddled for 3 minutes)
2 anchovies, rinsed and chopped, or
1 tablespoon anchovy paste
2 garlic cloves, crushed
1 teaspoon Dijon mustard
1 tablespoon Worcestershire sauce
1 1/2 cups olive oil
Juice of 1 lemon
1/3 cup grated Parmesan cheese
Salt and pepper to taste

Place the egg yolks, anchovies, garlic, Dijon mustard and Worcestershire sauce in a food processor or blender and process until smooth.

Add the olive oil in a fine stream until well blended, processing constantly. Thin the dressing with the lemon juice when it gets very thick. Pour the dressing into a bowl. Stir in the cheese, salt and pepper. Chill, covered, in the refrigerator until ready to use.

Makes 2 cups

Oriental Chicken Salad

Salad	Dressing
8 boneless skinless chicken breasts	$3/4$ cup vegetable oil
2 tablespoons olive oil	$1/2$ cup smooth natural peanut butter
Kosher salt and freshly ground pepper to taste	$1/3$ cup soy sauce
	$1/4$ cup cider vinegar
1 pound asparagus, trimmed and sliced diagonally into quarters	3 tablespoons dark sesame oil
	1 tablespoon honey
2 red bell peppers, julienned	2 garlic cloves, minced
4 scallions, sliced diagonally	2 teaspoons kosher salt
2 tablespoons sesame seeds, toasted	1 teaspoon freshly ground pepper
	1 teaspoon grated peeled fresh ginger

For the salad, preheat the oven to 350 degrees. Place the chicken on a baking sheet and rub with the olive oil. Season with salt and pepper. Roast for 35 to 40 minutes or until no longer pink. Cool and cut into bite-size pieces. Place the chicken in a large bowl. Blanch the asparagus in a saucepan of boiling salted water for 3 to 5 minutes; drain. Plunge the asparagus into ice water immediately to stop the cooking process; drain. Add the asparagus, bell peppers, scallions and sesame seeds to the chicken.

For the dressing, whisk together the vegetable oil, peanut butter, soy sauce, vinegar, sesame oil, honey, garlic, salt, pepper and ginger until combined. Pour over the chicken mixture and toss to coat. Chill, covered, in the refrigerator for several hours. Serve cold.

Serves 12

There are endless options for new combinations in this simple, flavorful main course salad.

- Serve on a bed of mixed greens.
- Substitute pork tenderloin strips or shrimp for the chicken.
- Toss in shredded bok choy for a little crunchiness.
- Add extra zing by sprinkling the salad with cayenne pepper to taste and then garnishing with slivered cucumber.
- Add more color by mixing in sliced yellow bell peppers.
- Create a crunchy top with a sprinkle of Chinese noodles, cashews, or spicy peanuts.
- Turn this lunch salad into a refreshing main course on a hot summer night by serving it on a cold bed of thin spaghetti that has been tossed with a small amount of sesame oil and minced garlic.

Grilled Asian Chicken Salad

Chicken
1/4 cup dry white wine
1 1/2 tablespoons soy sauce
Juice of 1/2 lemon
3 garlic cloves, crushed
1 tablespoon grated fresh ginger
2 teaspoons Dijon mustard
1/2 teaspoon red pepper flakes
3 pounds boneless skinless chicken breasts

Dressing
1 garlic clove
1 tablespoon sesame oil
2 tablespoons soy sauce
2 tablespoons sherry vinegar
1/3 cup olive oil

Salad
1 bunch fresh spinach leaves (about 10 ounces)
1 cup sugar snap peas
1/2 cup julienned red bell pepper
1/2 cup thinly sliced onion, separated into rings
1/2 cup snow peas
1/4 cup dried cranberries
1/2 teaspoon freshly ground pepper

For the chicken, whisk together the wine, soy sauce, lemon juice, garlic, ginger, Dijon mustard and red pepper flakes in a small bowl until combined. Pour over the chicken in a large bowl with a lid or sealable plastic bag. Marinate, covered, in the refrigerator for at least 3 hours or overnight. Remove the chicken from the marinade, discarding the marinade. Preheat the grill. Grill the chicken until no longer pink. Cool slightly and cut into bite-size pieces. Place the chicken in a large bowl.

For the dressing, place the garlic, sesame oil, soy sauce, vinegar and olive oil in a food processor and process until smooth. Pour over the chicken.

For the salad, add the spinach, sugar snap peas, bell pepper, onion, snow peas, dried cranberries and pepper to the chicken and toss.

Serves 6

West Indies Salad

1 onion, finely chopped
1 pound lump crab meat,
   drained and flaked
Salt and pepper to taste

1/2 cup vegetable oil
6 tablespoons cider vinegar
1/2 cup ice water
Lemon twists for garnish

Spread half the onion on the bottom of a large bowl. Cover with the crab meat and top with the remaining onion. Season with salt and pepper. Pour the oil, vinegar and ice water over the layers. Marinate, covered, in the refrigerator for 2 to 12 hours. Toss lightly before serving.

Spoon into an oversize martini glass and garnish with lemon.

Serves 4 to 6

Shrimp and Corn Salad

Salad
6 to 8 ears white sweet corn,
   cooked and cooled
1 to 1 1/2 pounds cooked shrimp,
   peeled and deveined
2 tomatoes, chopped
1 red bell pepper, chopped
1 red onion, chopped
1 cucumber, chopped

Dressing
1/2 cup sour cream
1/4 cup mayonnaise
2 tablespoons white vinegar
1/2 teaspoon celery seeds
1/2 teaspoon dry mustard
Shredded red leaf lettuce

For the salad, cut the corn from the ears into a large bowl. Add the shrimp, tomatoes, bell pepper, onion and cucumber and toss gently.

For the dressing, whisk together the sour cream, mayonnaise, vinegar, celery seeds and dry mustard in a small bowl until smooth. Pour over the shrimp mixture and mix well. Chill, covered, in the refrigerator for 1 hour or longer. Arrange the leaf lettuce on a platter and top with the salad.

Note: Two (12-ounce) cans of white corn, drained, may be substituted for the fresh corn.

Serves 6 to 8

Soups, Sandwiches & Pastas

Hearty favorites and delicious

one-course meals:

easy to create and easy to serve.

Autumn Carrot Bisque

6 tablespoons butter
2 pounds carrots, chopped
2 large Vidalia onions, chopped
1 tablespoon minced fresh ginger
2 teaspoons grated orange zest
1/2 teaspoon coriander
1/2 teaspoon nutmeg
5 cups vegetable broth or chicken broth
1 cup light cream or half-and-half
Salt to taste
Chopped parsley or crème fraîche for garnish

Melt the butter in a large saucepan. Add the carrots and onions and cook for 15 minutes or until the onions are translucent, stirring frequently. Stir in the ginger, orange zest, coriander and nutmeg. Add 2 cups of the broth and bring to a boil. Reduce the heat to medium-low and simmer for 30 minutes or until the carrots are tender. Ladle the carrot mixture, a small amount at a time, into a blender and process until smooth. Return the carrot purée to the pan and add the remaining broth. Simmer for 20 minutes. Stir in the cream and heat through. Season with salt. Ladle into serving bowls and garnish with parsley or crème fraîche.

Serves 6 to 8

Women's Build Gazpacho

2 cucumbers, peeled, seeded and chopped
2 red bell peppers, seeded and chopped
2 green bell peppers, seeded and chopped
2 tomatoes, seeded and chopped
1 onion, cut into wedges
3 garlic cloves
1/4 cup olive oil
1/4 teaspoon (or more) cumin
1 (46-ounce) can vegetable juice cocktail
3 tablespoons red wine vinegar
1 avocado, diced
Salt and cayenne pepper to taste
Chopped fresh cilantro
Sour cream

Combine half the cucumbers, half the bell peppers, half the tomatoes, the onion, garlic, olive oil and cumin in a food processor and purée until smooth. Pour the puréed mixture into a large bowl and stir in the remaining chopped vegetables. Add the vegetable juice cocktail, vinegar, avocado, salt, cayenne pepper and cilantro and mix well. Chill, covered, in the refrigerator for 2 to 3 hours. Ladle into serving bowls and top with sour cream.

Serves 8 to 10

CROWD-PLEASING RECIPES HAVE ALWAYS BEEN POPULAR in community service work, which is at the heart of the Marist School traditions. Whether preparing lunch for the Habitat for Humanity Women's Build volunteers or fixing dinner for Atlanta-area night shelters, Marist cooks create something special with their outreach efforts. Over the last century, generations of students, parents, faculty, and alumni have been involved in community work, from campus-wide blood drives for the American Red Cross to annual mission work in El Salvador and Honduras. Today, every Marist student participates in some type of hands-on community service, visibly supporting the school's mission to "form the whole person in the image of Christ."

Asparagus Soup

1/2 cup (1 stick) butter
4 onions, chopped
6 1/2 cups (about) chicken broth

3 pounds asparagus, trimmed, tips reserved and stalks coarsely chopped
Salt and white pepper to taste
Sour cream

Melt the butter in a large heavy saucepan over medium-high heat. Add the onions and sauté for 10 minutes or until tender. Add 6 cups of the broth and the chopped asparagus stalks and bring to a boil. Reduce the heat and cook for about 10 minutes or until the asparagus is tender. Cool slightly. Ladle the asparagus mixture, a small amount at a time, into a blender and process until smooth. Return the asparagus purée to the pan and add the remaining broth to reach the desired consistency. Season with salt and white pepper. The soup can be made 1 day ahead up to this point. Store, covered, in the refrigerator.

Heat the purée and add the reserved asparagus tips. Simmer for about 5 minutes or until tender.

Ladle into serving bowls and top with sour cream.

Serves 8 to 10

Simply Fresh Corn Soup

10 cobs sweet corn
3 to 4 teaspoons salt

1 onion, sliced
2 tablespoons olive oil

Cut the corn off the cobs into a large bowl, reserving the cobs. Place the corn cobs in a large stock pot and cover with water. Add the salt, onion and olive oil. Bring to a boil. Reduce the heat to medium and simmer for 30 to 40 minutes. Remove and discard the corn cobs. Return the mixture to a boil and add the corn kernels. Simmer for 10 to 20 minutes. Ladle the corn mixture, a small amount at a time, into a blender and process until smooth. Return the corn purée to the pot and heat through. Add water if the soup is too thick. Serve hot.

Serves 6 to 8

Acorn Squash Soup with Cinnamon-Sugar Croutons

Cinnamon-Sugar Croutons
4 slices white bread, crusts removed
2 tablespoons butter
4 teaspoons sugar
1 teaspoon ground cinnamon

Soup
4 acorn squash, halved lengthwise
and seeded
3 carrots, sliced
1 onion, sliced
2 tablespoons butter

1 tablespoon all-purpose flour
1 teaspoon salt
1 teaspoon pepper
2 (14-ounce) cans chicken broth
1/2 cup sherry
1/2 teaspoon nutmeg
1/8 teaspoon paprika
Dash of ground allspice
Dash of cayenne pepper
1 cup half-and-half
1 1/2 teaspoons sherry
Paprika

For the croutons, preheat the oven to 350 degrees. Cut the bread slices into 1/2-inch cubes. Melt the butter in a large skillet and add the bread, tossing to coat. Stir together the sugar and cinnamon in a small bowl and sprinkle over the bread cubes, tossing to coat. Spread the bread cubes on a baking parchment paper-lined baking sheet. Bake for 8 to 10 minutes or until crisp. The croutons can be prepared several days ahead. Store in an airtight container.

For the soup, preheat the oven to 350 degrees. Place the squash halves cut side down in a large shallow baking or broiler pan. Add 1 inch of hot water to the pan. Bake, covered, for 30 minutes or until tender. Scoop the pulp from the squash halves into a bowl, reserving the squash shells for serving the soup, if desired. Combine the carrots and onion with water to cover in a saucepan and bring to a boil. Reduce the heat and simmer, covered, for 15 minutes or until the vegetables are tender. Drain, reserving 1/3 cup of the cooking liquid. Add the carrot mixture and reserved liquid to the squash pulp and mix well. Ladle the squash mixture, a small amount at a time, into a blender and process until smooth.

Melt the butter in a Dutch oven or stockpot over low heat. Stir in the flour, salt and pepper until smooth. Cook for 1 minute, stirring constantly. Stir in the puréed vegetable mixture, broth, 1/2 cup sherry, the nutmeg, 1/8 teaspoon paprika, the allspice and cayenne pepper gradually. Bring to a boil.

Reduce the heat to low and simmer, covered, for 1 hour, stirring occasionally. Stir in the half-and-half and 1 1/2 teaspoons sherry and heat through. Ladle into the reserved squash shells or bowls and sprinkle with paprika. Top with the croutons.

Serves 8

Gorgonzola Tomato Soup

1 cup diced onion	2 (14-ounce) cans vegetable broth or
1/2 cup diced carrots	chicken broth
1/2 cup diced celery	1 1/2 cups cream, heavy cream or
4 garlic cloves, minced	half-and-half
2 tablespoons olive oil	1/4 to 1/2 cup (1 to 2 ounces)
1 cup white wine	Gorgonzola cheese
3 (28-ounce) cans crushed	Chopped fresh basil leaves
Italian tomatoes	Salt and pepper to taste

Sauté the onion, carrots, celery and garlic in the olive oil in a large saucepan until tender. Add the wine and simmer until most of the liquid has evaporated. Add the tomatoes and broth. Simmer for 30 minutes. Ladle the tomato mixture, a small amount at a time, into a blender or food processor and process until smooth. Return to the saucepan and bring to a boil. Reduce the heat and add the cream and cheese. Heat until the cheese melts, stirring constantly. Ladle the soup into serving bowls and top with generous amounts of basil. Season with salt and pepper.

Serves 16

Tuscan Soup

3 (3-ounce) links Italian sausage,	1 (10-ounce) package fresh spinach
casings removed, or 1 1/2 pounds	leaves, chopped, or 1 (10-ounce)
Italian bulk pork sausage	package frozen chopped spinach,
1 onion, chopped	thawed and drained
6 cups chicken broth	1/4 cup evaporated milk, or 1/2 cup cream
2 large potatoes, cubed	or heavy cream
	Salt to taste

Crumble the sausage into a large skillet and add the onion. Cook over medium heat until the sausage is no longer pink; drain or place in a colander and rinse under cold water. Combine the sausage mixture, broth and potatoes in a large saucepan. Bring to a boil. Reduce the heat and cook until the potatoes are tender. Add the spinach and heat through. Remove from the heat and stir in the evaporated milk. Season with salt.

Serves 6

White Lightning Chili

1 large onion, chopped
4 ribs celery, chopped
2 garlic cloves, minced
2 to 3 tablespoons vegetable oil
4 (14-ounce) cans chicken broth
4 (16-ounce) cans navy beans,
    drained and rinsed
5 cups chopped cooked chicken breasts
2 (4-ounce) cans diced green
    chiles, drained

1 cup water
1 tablespoon ground cumin
1 tablespoon Italian seasoning
1 tablespoon white pepper
1 teaspoon salt
Condiments: sour cream, salsa, shredded
    Monterey Jack cheese, chopped green
    onions and crushed tortilla chips

Sauté the onion, celery and garlic in the oil in a large saucepan or stock pot until tender. Add the broth and 3 cans of the beans. Purée the remaining beans in a blender and add to the chili. Add the chicken, green chiles, water, cumin, Italian seasoning, white pepper and salt. Bring to a boil. Reduce the heat and simmer for 1 hour, stirring occasionally. Ladle into serving bowls and pass the condiments for topping.

Serves 12

BACON-WRAPPED BREADSTICKS

Bacon-wrapped breadsticks are a delicious accompaniment to any type of chili. You will need 30 slices bacon (approximately 1 pound), 1/3 cup firmly packed light brown sugar, 30 long thin breadsticks (grissini), and 3 tablespoons pure chili powder. Let the bacon stand at room temperature for about 10 minutes or until slightly softened. Wrap 1 slice of bacon gently in a spiral pattern around each breadstick and arrange on a tray. Breadsticks may be wrapped 4 hours ahead and chilled, covered, in the refrigerator.

Preheat the oven to 350 degrees. Combine the brown sugar and chili powder in a long shallow dish and mix well. Press out any lumps with the back of a fork. Roll each breadstick gently in the mixture, coating the bacon well, and arrange 1/2-inch apart on the rack of a broiler pan. Bake the breadsticks for 20 minutes or until the coating is caramelized and the bacon is deep golden brown. Loosen the breadsticks gently from the rack with a metal spatula and cool for 10 to 15 minutes or until firm. Serve the breadsticks at room temperature.

Southwest Chicken Soup

1/2 cup diced onion
2 garlic cloves, minced
1 teaspoon ground cumin
1/2 teaspoon chili powder
1/8 teaspoon cayenne pepper
2 tablespoons olive oil
1 (14-ounce) can chicken broth
1 (14-ounce) can corn
1 (14-ounce) can Mexican-style stewed tomatoes
1 (15-ounce) can black beans, drained and rinsed
8 ounces boneless skinless chicken breasts
6 tablespoons sour cream
2 tablespoons chopped fresh cilantro
Tortilla chips, broken

Cook the onion, garlic, cumin, chili powder and cayenne pepper in the olive oil in a Dutch oven or stockpot for 1 1/2 minutes or until the spices are fragrant, stirring constantly. Add the broth, corn, tomatoes and beans and bring to a boil. Add the chicken and bring to a boil. Reduce the heat to medium and cook, covered, for 10 minutes or until the chicken is no longer pink. Remove the chicken to a cutting board and shred. Return the chicken to the soup and heat for 5 minutes. Ladle into serving bowls and top with the sour cream, cilantro and tortilla chips.

Serves 6 to 8

Seafood Chowder

2 (10-ounce) frozen lobster tails, thawed
8 cups frozen yellow corn, thawed
1¼ cups low-salt chicken broth
8 slices bacon, chopped
2 cups chopped onions
¾ cup finely chopped peeled carrots
⅔ cup finely chopped celery
¼ teaspoon cayenne pepper

3 cups clam juice
1¾ cups low-salt chicken broth
1½ cups cream or heavy cream
Salt and pepper to taste
6 tablespoons sour cream, at room
  temperature
2 tablespoons butter
3 tablespoons chopped fresh chives

Cook the lobster tails in a large pot of boiling water for 6 minutes; drain and cool. Cut the lobster shells open with kitchen shears and remove the meat. Discard the shells and cut the meat into bite-size pieces. Combine 4 cups of the corn and 1¼ cups broth in a food processor and purée.

Sauté the bacon in a large stockpot over medium heat for 5 minutes or until crisp. Remove the bacon to paper towels to drain. Pour off all but 3 tablespoons of the drippings. Add the onions to the drippings and sauté for 5 minutes or until light golden brown. Add the remaining 4 cups corn and sauté for 3 minutes. Add the carrot, celery and cayenne pepper. Cook for 45 minutes or until the vegetables are tender.

Add the clam juice and 1¾ cups broth. Bring to boil and simmer for 10 minutes. Stir in the corn purée and the cream. Simmer for 5 minutes. Season with salt and pepper. Remove the soup from the heat and stir in the sour cream. Melt the butter in a medium nonstick skillet over medium heat. Add the lobster meat and sauté for 2 minutes or until heated through. Ladle the chowder into serving bowls and add the lobster meat, bacon and chives.

*Note: One pound cooked lobster meat, cut into bite-size pieces, or 1 pound crab meat or cooked shrimp, peeled and deveined, can be substituted for the lobster tails.
The lobster, bacon and chowder base can be made 1 day ahead. Store separately, covered, in the refrigerator. Bring the bacon to room temperature and bring the chowder to a simmer before continuing as above.*

Serves 8

Portobello Mushroom Stew

Mushroom Stock

6 ounces portobello mushroom stems
1 unpeeled carrot, sliced
1 small leek, sliced lengthwise
1 unpeeled small onion, chopped
1 rib celery, sliced
1 unpeeled garlic clove
1 sprig parsley
1 bay leaf
1 teaspoon whole peppercorns
1 teaspoon fresh thyme leaves
6 cups water

Stew

8 ounces rutabagas or turnips,
  cut into chunks
8 ounces parsnips cut into chunks
8 ounces carrots, cut into chunks
8 ounces shallots, cut into halves
6 tablespoons olive oil
$2^{1}/_{2}$ pounds portobello mushroom
  caps, quartered
$1^{1}/_{2}$ tablespoons minced fresh
  rosemary leaves
$1^{1}/_{2}$ tablespoons minced fresh
  thyme leaves
$1^{1}/_{2}$ teaspoons minced garlic
$^{1}/_{2}$ cup plus 2 tablespoons red wine
1 (16-ounce) can crushed tomatoes
$^{1}/_{4}$ cup water
$^{1}/_{4}$ cup all-purpose flour
$1^{1}/_{2}$ teaspoons salt
$^{1}/_{2}$ teaspoon pepper
1 tablespoon lemon juice

For the stock, combine the mushroom stems, carrot, leek, onion, celery, garlic, parsley, bay leaf, peppercorns and thyme in a large saucepan or stockpot. Add the water and bring to a boil over high heat. Reduce the heat to low and simmer, uncovered, for 1 hour or until the liquid is reduced to 4 cups. Strain and reserve 2 cups of the stock for the stew. Reserve the remaining stock for another use. Store, covered, in the refrigerator or freezer.

For the stew, cook the rutabagas, parsnips, carrots and shallots in the olive oil in a large Dutch oven or stockpot over medium-high heat for 12 to 15 minutes or until brown and caramelized, stirring frequently. Add the mushroom caps, rosemary, thyme and garlic and cook for 10 minutes, stirring occasionally. Add the wine, stirring to deglaze the pan. Add the tomatoes and 2 cups reserved mushroom stock. Bring to a boil. Reduce the heat and simmer, covered, for 45 minutes. Whisk together the water and flour in a small bowl until smooth. Stir the flour mixture into the stew and cook, uncovered, for 15 minutes longer, stirring frequently. Season with the salt, pepper and lemon juice. Serve over mashed potatoes, polenta or your favorite pasta.

Makes 12 cups

Chicken and Pesto Sandwiches

Basil Olive Pesto
1 large garlic clove
1 cup packed fresh basil leaves
1 cup packed fresh flat-leaf parsley
1/3 cup pine nuts
1/4 cup olive oil
1/4 cup kalamata olives or other
  brine-cured black olives, pitted and
    finely chopped

Sandwiches
3 ounces sun-dried tomatoes
  (not oil-pack)
1 (20-inch) loaf Italian or French bread
2 or 3 grilled chicken breasts,
  thinly sliced, or 1 pound smoked
  chicken breast, sliced
1/2 bunch (about 1 cup) arugula,
  trimmed

For the pesto, process the garlic in a food processor until finely chopped. Add the basil, parsley and pine nuts and process until finely chopped. Add the olive oil in a steady stream, processing constantly until smooth. Pour the pesto into a bowl and stir in the olives. The pesto can be made up to 5 days ahead. Store, tightly covered, in the refrigerator.

For the sandwiches, pour enough boiling water over the tomatoes in a bowl to cover and let stand for 20 to 30 minutes. Drain the tomatoes and pat dry. Slice the bread loaf diagonally into 4 pieces. Slice each piece in half horizontally. Spread the cut sides of the bread with the pesto. Top the bottom bread slices with the tomatoes, chicken, arugula and the bread tops. Serve warm.

Serves 4

This simple sandwich will make any cook look like a gourmet. Easy to prepare and present, consider these variations when planning your menu:

- Assemble sandwich as described, without the arugula. Grill or toast in a pan and then add the arugula immediately before serving.
- Add extra zip to the pesto with a dash of cayenne pepper.
- Substitute sliced fresh tomatoes and spinach leaves.
- Add a slice of smoked mozzarella or provolone.
- Substitute a 9-grain baguette for an earthy flavor.
- Add a slice of imported prosciutto.
- Use sun-dried tomato pesto spread liberally on the bread.

Grilled Havarti Sandwich

2 slices sourdough bread or 5-grain bread
Honey mustard to taste
Several slices Havarti cheese with dill
1 package broccoli slaw

Spread 1 side of each bread slice with the honey mustard. Arrange 3 or 4 slices of the cheese on 1 bread slice. Top with the slaw and another cheese slice. Cover with the remaining bread, mustard-side down. Toast in a panini press or grill in a small amount of butter or vegetable oil in a skillet until golden brown on both sides.

Serves 1

Tailgate Sandwich

1 (6-ounce) jar roasted red peppers,
cut into strips
1/4 cup olive oil
1/4 cup balsamic vinegar
2 garlic cloves, minced
2 round rye or pumpernickel
bread loaves
3 to 4 tablespoons Dijon mustard

12 slices Genoa salami (8 ounces)
8 ounces fresh spinach leaves
12 slices provolone cheese (8 ounces)
12 thin slices red onion
12 thin slices cooked turkey breast
(8 ounces)
12 thin slices cooked ham (8 ounces)

Combine the peppers, olive oil, vinegar and garlic in a bowl and mix well. Marinate, covered, in the refrigerator for 1 hour or overnight. Cut off the tops of the bread loaves and reserve. Remove the inside of the bread loaves, leaving a 1/2-inch shell. Spread the inside of the loaves with the Dijon mustard. Layer the salami, spinach, drained marinated peppers, cheese, onion, turkey and ham in each loaf. Replace the tops of the loaves. Wrap tightly in plastic wrap then in foil. Chill in the refrigerator overnight. Unwrap and cut each loaf into 5 or 6 wedges.

Serves 10 to 12

Four-Cheese Crepes with Tomato Sauce

Crepes
1 to 1¹/4 cups water
1 cup all-purpose flour
2 eggs
¹/8 teaspoon salt
Vegetable oil

Tomato Sauce
1 (28- to 32-ounce) can whole tomatoes
1 small onion, finely chopped
3 garlic cloves, finely chopped
¹/4 cup extra-virgin olive oil
1 teaspoon salt
Fresh basil or oregano to taste

Filling
1 pound ricotta cheese
1 cup (4 ounces) shredded
  mozzarella cheese
¹/4 cup (1 ounce) grated
  Parmesan cheese
¹/4 cup (1 ounce) grated Romano cheese
1 egg
2 tablespoons chopped fresh parsley
¹/2 teaspoon garlic salt
¹/2 teaspoon pepper

For the crepes, whisk together 1 cup water, the flour, eggs and salt in a bowl until blended. Add additional water if needed for a thin pourable consistency. Heat a small heavy skillet over low heat until hot. Brush the pan lightly with oil. Stir the batter and ladle 3 to 4 tablespoons into the pan, tilting to coat the bottom evenly. Cook the crepe for 1 minute or until set, but not brown. Loosen the edge of the crepe; turn over and cook the other side until set. Repeat with the remaining batter. The crepes can be made ahead. Stack between sheets of waxed paper and cool completely. Wrap tightly and store in the refrigerator for up to 3 days or freeze for up to 1 month. Bring to room temperature before using.

For the tomato sauce, place the tomatoes in a food processor and process until coarsely puréed. Sauté the onion and garlic in the olive oil in a heavy saucepan until tender. Add the tomatoes and simmer for about 40 minutes or until slightly thickened. Season with the salt and basil.

For the filling, preheat the oven to 350 degrees. Combine the ricotta cheese, mozzarella cheese, Parmesan cheese, Romano cheese, egg, parsley, garlic salt and pepper in a bowl and mix well. Divide the filling equally among the crepes and roll up. Place the crepes in a greased 9×13-inch baking dish and top with 1 cup of the tomato sauce. Bake for 40 minutes. Serve with additional tomato sauce on the side.

Serves 6

VARIATION: One 10-ounce package frozen chopped spinach, thawed and well-drained, can be added to the cheese filling. One or more of these ingredients can be added to the tomato sauce: red pepper flakes, puréed sun-dried tomatoes, chopped red and green bell peppers, sliced mushrooms, and/or freshly grated Parmesan or Romano cheese.

Asian Angel Hair Pasta

Sesame Dressing	Pasta
1/4 cup soy sauce	1/4 cup pine nuts
3 tablespoons rice vinegar	3 quarts water
2 tablespoons sesame oil	1 tablespoon salt
1 tablespoon sugar	12 ounces angel hair pasta
	1 pound shrimp, peeled and deveined
	8 ounces snow peas
	1/4 cup chopped fresh cilantro
	1/4 cup thinly sliced green onions
	Grated fresh ginger for garnish

For the dressing, whisk together the soy sauce, vinegar, sesame oil and sugar in small bowl until blended.

For the pasta, toast the pine nuts in a Dutch oven over medium heat for 5 minutes or until golden brown, stirring frequently. Combine the water and salt in a large saucepan and bring to a boil. Stir in the pasta and cook for 3 minutes. Stir in the shrimp and snow peas. Cook until the shrimp turn pink. Drain well and place in a large bowl. Add the cilantro, green onions and dressing and toss. Sprinkle with the pine nuts. Serve hot or chilled. Garnish with ginger.

Serves 6 to 8

Angel Hair Pasta with Vegetables

2 bell peppers, diced	8 fresh basil leaves, chopped
1/2 red onion, minced	Juice of 1 lime
7 tomatoes, seeded and chopped	8 ounces angel hair pasta
2 (14-ounce) cans artichoke hearts, drained and quartered	4 ounces goat cheese, sliced
	1/4 cup pine nuts

Combine the bell peppers, onion, tomatoes, artichoke hearts and basil in a large bowl and mix well. Sprinkle with the lime juice and let stand at room temperature for 1 hour. Cook the pasta to al dente using the package directions; drain. Place the pasta in a large serving bowl and top with the cheese and the vegetable mixture; toss. Sprinkle with the pine nuts.

Serves 8 to 10

Grilled Chicken Farfalle

1/2 cup soy sauce
2 tablespoons grated fresh ginger
2 garlic cloves, minced
3 whole boneless chicken breasts
2 ears sweet corn, cooked
1 pound farfalle pasta,
cooked and drained
1 (12-ounce) jar roasted red peppers,
sliced and drained

1/2 cup (2 ounces) crumbled feta cheese
1/2 red onion, sliced
8 ounces grape tomatoes, cut into halves
3 tablespoons balsamic vinegar
1/2 cup olive oil
3 tablespoons chopped fresh basil leaves
Salt and pepper to taste

Combine the soy sauce, ginger and garlic in a small saucepan and bring to a boil. Remove from the heat and cool for 30 minutes. Pour over the chicken in a large bowl or sealable plastic bag. Marinate, covered, in the refrigerator for 1 hour. Remove the chicken from the marinade; discard the marinade. Grill over hot coals until the chicken is no longer pink; cool. Chop into bite-size pieces and place in a large bowl. Cut the corn off the cobs and add to the chicken. Add the pasta, peppers, cheese, onion and tomatoes and toss. Whisk together the vinegar and olive oil in a small bowl. Add the basil to the chicken mixture and season with salt and pepper. Pour the vinaigrette over and toss. Serve immediately.

Serves 8

Spinach Sausage Fettuccini

1/4 cup olive oil
4 ounces hot or mild Italian sausage,
casings removed
8 ounces mushrooms, sliced
2 bunches fresh spinach, trimmed, or
1 (10-ounce) bag spinach leaves
2 teaspoons minced garlic

1/4 cup coarsely chopped walnuts
2 cups cream or heavy cream
4 ounces Gorgonzola cheese
2 teaspoons Dijon mustard
Salt and pepper to taste
1 pound fettuccini, cooked and drained

Heat the olive oil in a large skillet over medium-high heat. Add the sausage and cook for 5 minutes or until no longer pink, stirring until crumbly. Remove the sausage with a slotted spoon to a bowl. Add the mushrooms to the drippings in the skillet and sauté for 2 minutes. Add the spinach and sauté until wilted. Add the garlic and walnuts and cook for 1 minute. Stir in the cream and cheese and bring to a boil. Reduce the heat and simmer for 10 minutes or until thickened to a sauce consistency, stirring occasionally. Add the sausage and Dijon mustard and mix well; heat through. Season with salt and pepper. Pour the sauce over the fettuccini and toss gently.

Serves 4 to 6

Penne Pancetta

1 tablespoon olive oil	1 pound penne
1 large Vidalia onion, diced	1 tablespoon sherry vinegar
1 large red onion, diced	Freshly ground pepper
12 ounces pancetta, diced	Additional sherry vinegar
1 garlic clove, sliced	

Heat the olive oil in a large skillet over medium-high heat. Add the onions and cook, covered, for 5 minutes. Stir in the pancetta and garlic and cook, uncovered, over low heat until brown and caramelized, stirring occasionally. Cook the pasta using the package directions; drain and place in a large bowl. Stir 1 tablespoon vinegar into the pancetta mixture and heat through. Pour over the pasta and toss to coat. Season with pepper and additional vinegar. Serve immediately.

Serves 6 to 8

Asparagus Cream Penne

1/3 cup pistachios	1 cup half-and-half
1 pound asparagus, trimmed and cut into thirds	1/4 cup cream or heavy cream
1 garlic clove, peeled and halved	1 1/2 teaspoons kosher salt
1/4 cup (1/2 stick) unsalted butter	1 pound penne
1/4 teaspoon white pepper	1/2 cup (2 ounces) freshly grated Parmigiano-Reggiano cheese
1/3 cup dry white wine	

Preheat the oven to 350 degrees. Place the pistachios on a baking sheet and toast for 5 to 7 minutes. Cool and chop the pistachios. Cook the asparagus in a large stockpot of boiling salted water over medium-high heat for about 3 minutes or until tender. Remove the asparagus and reserve the cooking water. Sauté the garlic in the butter in a large skillet over medium heat just until the edges of the garlic begin to brown. Remove and discard the garlic. Add the asparagus and white pepper to the butter. Increase the heat to high and add the wine. Cook for 1 minute, stirring constantly. Reduce the heat to medium and stir in the half-and-half and cream. Simmer for 2 minutes. Season with the salt. Keep warm. Cook the pasta in the reserved asparagus water using the package directions; drain and return to the stockpot. Add the asparagus mixture to the pasta and cook over low heat, stirring constantly. Add the cheese and stir until melted. Remove to a platter or individual serving plates and sprinkle with the pistachios. Serve immediately.

Serves 4 to 6

Shrimp and Tomato Risotto

5 garlic cloves, chopped, or
1 tablespoon jarred garlic
2 tablespoons olive oil
24 large shrimp, peeled, deveined and
tails removed (about 1 1/2 pounds)
4 cups chicken stock
1 onion, chopped
1 leek, thinly sliced
1/4 cup olive oil
2 cups arborio rice

1/2 to 1 cup white wine
10 plum tomatoes, peeled and chopped,
or 2 cups canned diced tomatoes
1/4 cup (1/2 stick) butter
1/2 cup (2 ounces) grated Parmesan
cheese or Romano cheese
1/4 cup chopped parsley
2 tablespoons chopped fresh thyme
leaves or basil leaves
Salt and pepper to taste

Sauté the garlic in 2 tablespoons olive oil in a large skillet over medium-high heat until the garlic is just beginning to brown. Add the shrimp and sauté until they turn pink. Remove from the heat. Pour the stock into a saucepan and bring to a boil. Reduce the heat and hold the stock at a simmer.

Sauté the onion and leek in 1/4 cup olive oil in a large saucepan over medium-high heat until translucent. Add the rice and sauté for 3 minutes. Add the wine and cook until absorbed, stirring constantly.

Add the hot stock 1/2 cup at a time, allowing the stock to be absorbed before the next addition. Taste the rice after 2 cups of stock have been added to determine when the rice is cooked al dente. Not all of the stock may be needed. Add the shrimp and tomatoes with the last of the stock, cooking until the stock is absorbed, stirring constantly. Remove from the heat and add the butter, cheese, parsley and thyme. Season with salt and pepper and serve immediately.

Note: The shrimp shells can be added to the simmering chicken stock for a more pronounced shrimp flavor. Be careful not to add any shells to the risotto.

Serves 6

Basic Bolognese Sauce

1 onion, finely chopped
1 garlic clove, peeled and minced
1/4 cup extra-virgin olive oil
1 rib celery, finely chopped
1 pound ground beef chuck or ground round
1 (28-ounce) can crushed tomatoes
1/4 cup finely chopped flat-leaf parsley
8 fresh basil leaves, chopped
1/2 teaspoon salt
1/2 teaspoon freshly ground pepper
1/4 cup (1 ounce) freshly grated pecorino Romano cheese
1 pound pasta, cooked and drained

Sauté the onion and garlic in the olive oil in a large skillet over medium heat for 8 minutes or until tender. Add the celery and sauté for 5 minutes longer. Increase the heat to high and add the beef. Sauté until the meat is no longer pink, stirring until crumbly. Add the tomatoes, parsley, basil, salt and pepper. Cook over medium-low heat for 30 minutes or until the sauce thickens. Stir in the cheese and taste, adding more salt and pepper if needed. Serve over the hot pasta.

Serves 4

Lo Mein Noodles with Broccoli and Chicken

1/4 cup chicken broth
3 tablespoons low-sodium soy sauce
2 tablespoons rice vinegar
1 teaspoon honey
1/2 teaspoon crushed red pepper
12 ounces chicken breast tenders, cut into bite-size pieces
2 tablespoons vegetable oil
1 1/2 teaspoons dark sesame oil
1 teaspoon vegetable oil
3 cups quartered mushrooms
3 cups broccoli florets
1 cup red bell pepper strips
2 garlic cloves, minced
1 cup snow peas
1 (8-ounce) can sliced water chestnuts, drained
6 ounces lo mein noodles, cooked and drained
Chow mein noodles for garnish

Whisk together the broth, soy sauce, vinegar, honey and crushed red pepper in a small bowl until blended. Stir-fry the chicken in 2 tablespoons vegetable oil in a large nonstick skillet over medium-high heat for 4 minutes or until the chicken is no longer pink. Remove the chicken from the pan and keep warm. Add the sesame oil and 1 teaspoon vegetable oil to the pan and heat over medium-high heat. Add the mushrooms, broccoli, bell pepper, garlic, snow peas and water chestnuts. Stir-fry for 4 minutes or until the broccoli is tender-crisp. Return the chicken to the pan and stir in the broth mixture; heat through. Serve over the noodles. Serve with additional soy sauce, if desired. Garnish with chow mein noodles.

Serves 4

Seafood & Fish

Fantastic seafood and fish

selections with a distinctive flair

are ideal for entertaining.

Seared Scallops with Marinated Endive

3 tablespoons sherry vinegar
1¹/2 tablespoons canola oil
1¹/2 tablespoons minced shallot
2 small heads Belgian endive, sliced diagonally
1 tablespoon canola oil
6 sea scallops (about 10 ounces)
1 teaspoon curry powder
6 ounces haricots verts or other young tender green beans,
trimmed and cut into 2-inch pieces
2 teaspoons white truffle oil
1/4 cup chopped fresh chives

Whisk together the vinegar, 1½ tablespoons canola oil and the shallot in a small bowl until combined. Place the endive in a medium bowl and add 2 tablespoons of the vinaigrette, tossing to coat. Let stand at room temperature for 20 minutes. Heat 1 tablespoon canola oil in a large heavy skillet over medium heat. Sprinkle the scallops with the curry powder and add to the skillet. Cook for 3 minutes; turn over and cook for about 2 minutes longer or until the scallops are almost opaque in the center.

Blanch the haricots verts for 3 to 4 minutes. Arrange 3 scallops around the edge of 2 individual serving plates. Divide the haricots verts into 6 bundles and arrange 3 bundles on each plate between the scallops. Mound half of the endive in the center of each plate. Drizzle the remaining vinaigrette over the scallops and green beans. Drizzle 1 teaspoon of the truffle oil over each salad and sprinkle with the chives.

Serves 2

Rustic Firecracker Shrimp

Rustic Rub
2¹/₂ tablespoons paprika
2 tablespoons garlic powder
2 tablespoons salt
1 tablespoon black pepper
1 tablespoon cayenne pepper
1 tablespoon onion powder
1 tablespoon dried oregano
1 tablespoon dried thyme

Shrimp
1 pound large shrimp, split, peeled and deveined
Salt and cracked pepper to taste
1 teaspoon vegetable oil
Juice of 2 lemons
1 cup cream or heavy cream
2 tablespoons butter
Hot pepper sauce to taste
2 tablespoons chopped fresh parsley
Hot cooked jasmine rice

For the rub, combine the paprika, garlic powder, salt, black pepper, cayenne pepper, onion powder, oregano and thyme in a bowl and mix well. Store tightly covered.

For the shrimp, combine the shrimp, desired amount of the rub, salt and cracked pepper in a large bowl and toss to coat. Sauté the shrimp in the oil in a large skillet or sauté pan over high heat for 1 to 2 minutes. Add the lemon juice, stirring to deglaze the pan. Stir in the cream, butter and hot sauce. Cook over high heat for 3 to 5 minutes or until the liquid is slightly reduced. Remove from the heat and stir in the parsley. Serve over rice.

Serves 4

Shrimp and Grits

Grits
1 cup uncooked grits
2 cups (8 ounces) shredded sharp Cheddar cheese
2 eggs, beaten
1/8 teaspoon paprika

Shrimp
1/2 cup Worcestershire sauce
1/2 cup soy sauce
6 tablespoons butter
1/4 cup fresh lemon juice
1/4 cup ketchup
1 tablespoon dried crushed parsley flakes
1 teaspoon garlic powder
1 teaspoon oregano
1 1/2 to 2 pounds shrimp, peeled and deveined

For the grits, preheat the oven to 375 degrees. Cook the grits using the package directions. Stir in 1 1/2 cups of the cheese. Add the eggs and pepper and mix well. Pour into a greased 1 1/2-quart shallow baking dish or 8×8-inch baking dish. Top with the remaining 1/2 cup cheese and sprinkle with paprika. Bake for 20 minutes.

For the shrimp, combine the Worcestershire sauce, soy sauce, butter, lemon juice, ketchup, parsley flakes, garlic powder and oregano in a large skillet and simmer for about 20 minutes. Add the shrimp and cook for 8 minutes or until the shrimp turn pink. Serve over the baked grits.

Serves 6 to 8

Savannah Spicy Shrimp

1/2 cup chicken broth
1/4 cup white wine or dry sherry
1/4 cup soy sauce
4 teaspoons red wine vinegar
1 tablespoon chili paste with garlic, or to taste
2 teaspoons sugar
2 tablespoons cornstarch
3 tablespoons vegetable oil

2 garlic cloves, crushed (optional)
1/2 green bell pepper, cubed
1/2 red bell pepper, cubed
1/2 yellow bell pepper, cubed
1 to 2 pounds large shrimp, peeled and deveined
1 bunch green onions, sliced into 1/2-inch pieces

Whisk together the broth, wine, soy sauce, vinegar, chili paste and sugar in a bowl until smooth. Whisk in the cornstarch until smooth. Heat the oil in a large wok or skillet over medium heat (350 degrees). Add the garlic and bell peppers and stir-fry for 1 minute. Add the shrimp and stir-fry until the shrimp turn pink. Add the sauce and stir-fry until the mixture is slightly thickened. Sprinkle with the green onions and serve.

Note: Chili paste is available at gourmet and specialty food stores.

Serves 4

Grilled Halibut with Summer Vegetables

2 1/2 cups coarsely chopped red onions
1 tablespoon olive oil
1 1/2 pounds plum tomatoes, cubed
1 yellow bell pepper, julienned
6 ounces yellow squash, diced
6 ounces zucchini, diced
2/3 cup fresh corn kernels, or frozen corn, thawed

3 tablespoons julienned fresh basil leaves
3 tablespoons chopped fresh parsley
4 (6-ounce) halibut steaks
Salt and pepper to taste
1 tablespoon fresh lime juice
2 tablespoons julienned fresh basil leaves

Sauté the onions in the olive oil in a large nonstick skillet over medium heat for 5 minutes. Add the tomatoes and bell pepper and sauté for 3 minutes. Stir in the squash, zucchini, corn, 3 tablespoons basil and the parsley. Simmer, covered, for 3 minutes or until the zucchini is tender-crisp. Season the halibut steaks with salt and pepper. Coat the grill rack with vegetable oil. Preheat the grill to medium. Grill the steaks for about 8 minutes or until opaque, turning once. Remove the steaks to a serving platter. Drizzle with the lime juice. Spoon the sautéed vegetables over the fish and sprinkle with 2 tablespoons basil.

Serves 4

FABULOUS GRILLED FISH FILLETS

Grilled fish fillets topped with a special sauce are perfect for warm weather entertaining. Start with the freshest fillets available and serve with one of the toppings suggested for an easy healthy entrée.

SALMON
6-ounce fillet with skin

Preheat the grill to medium. Brush the fillet lightly with olive oil and season with salt and pepper. Grill the salmon flesh-side down for 7 minutes or until opaque. Turn the salmon and grill skin-side down for 2 to 3 minutes. Slide a spatula between the skin and flesh and transfer to a plate.

SWORDFISH or HALIBUT
6- to 8-ounce fillet, 1 inch thick

Preheat the grill to high. Brush the fillet lightly with olive oil and season with kosher salt and freshly ground pepper. Grill for 8 to 10 minutes, or until opaque in the center, turning once halfway through the cooking process.

SEA BASS, GROUPER, or RED SNAPPER
6-ounce skinless fillet, 1 inch thick

Preheat the grill to high. Brush the fillet lightly with olive oil and season with kosher salt and freshly ground pepper. Grill for 5 to 7 minutes until opaque throughout, turning once halfway through the cooking process.

TUNA
Sushi-grade 6-ounce steaks, 1 1/2 inches thick

Preheat the grill to high. Brush both sides of the tuna lightly with olive oil and season with kosher salt and freshly ground pepper. Grill with the lid open for 3 to 4 minutes, turning once halfway through the cooking process. The surface should be scored and the center still red when the cooking is complete.

Roasted Yellow Beet Relish

6 large yellow beets
1 1/2 tablespoons olive oil
Salt and freshly ground pepper to taste
2 sprigs fresh thyme
1 bay leaf
1/2 cup water

1 shallot, minced
1 tablespoon olive oil
2 oranges, segmented, or 1 can mandarin
    oranges, drained
1 teaspoon honey
2 tablespoons pine nuts

Preheat the oven to 400 degrees. Wash the beets and cut off the stems. Place the beets on a large rectangle of aluminum foil on a flat working surface. Drizzle the beets with 1 1/2 tablespoons olive oil and season with salt and pepper. Add the thyme sprigs and bay leaf. Lift the corners of the aluminum foil and wrap tightly. Bake for 1 to 2 hours, or until the beets are soft when pricked with a knife. Unwrap and discard the thyme and bay leaf; let cool. Peel and dice the beets. (Can be refrigerated at this point.) Place the diced beets and the water in a pot over medium heat.

Cover and cook until the water and beets are hot; drain. Add the shallot, 1 tablespoon olive oil, the orange segments and honey and mix well. Return to the heat and bring to a boil, stirring constantly. Remove from the heat and stir in the pine nuts.

Mango and Cucumber Salsa

2 cups diced mangoes
    (about 1 1/2 pounds)
1 cup diced unpeeled English cucumbers
3/4 cup diced red bell pepper
1/3 cup chopped fresh cilantro

2 tablespoons fresh lime juice
2 tablespoons apricot preserves
1 teaspoon chopped canned chipotle chiles
Salt and pepper to taste

Combine the mangoes, cucumber, bell pepper, cilantro, lime juice, apricot preserves and chiles in a medium bowl and mix well. Season with salt and pepper to taste. It may be prepared 2 hours ahead. Chill, covered, in the refrigerator. Stir to blend just before serving.

Lemon Shallot Vinaigrette

6 tablespoons olive oil
1/3 cup minced shallots
2 tablespoons fresh lemon juice

1 tablespoon sherry vinegar
2 teaspoons packed lemon zest
Salt and pepper to taste

Whisk the olive oil, shallots, lemon juice, sherry vinegar and lemon zest in a small bowl and mix well. Season with salt and pepper to taste.

Horseradish-Crusted Salmon

4 (6-ounce) salmon fillets or grouper fillets
Salt and pepper to taste
3 tablespoons horseradish
3 tablespoons Dijon mustard
2 cups Italian-seasoned bread crumbs
Vegetable oil for sautéing

Season the fish with salt and pepper on both sides. Combine the horseradish and Dijon mustard in a small bowl and mix well. Brush onto the tops of the fillets, coating completely. Dip the horseradish-coated sides of the fillets in the bread crumbs, coating completely. Heat a large nonstick skillet or sauté pan over medium heat and add enough oil to coat the bottom. Place the fillets, coated-side down, in the pan and cook until golden brown. Turn the fish and cook until opaque.

Serves 4

Italian Sea Bass

1/2 onion, chopped
1 (14-ounce) can diced tomatoes with Italian seasonings, drained
1/2 cup white wine
1 teaspoon crushed red pepper flakes
1 (1 1/3-pound) sea bass fillet or other whitefish fillet, cut into 4 pieces

Sauté the onion in a lightly oiled large sauté pan or skillet for 2 to 3 minutes or until tender. Add the tomatoes, wine and red pepper flakes and simmer for 5 minutes, stirring occasionally. Add the fish. Cook, covered, for 7 to 10 minutes or until the fish flakes easily. Spoon the sauce over the fish. Serve with hot cooked rice, if desired.

Serves 4

Snapper with Banana Salsa

Salsa
2 bananas, chopped
1/2 cup chopped green bell pepper
1/2 cup chopped red bell pepper
3 scallions, chopped
3 tablespoons chopped fresh cilantro, or to taste
2 tablespoons light brown sugar
3 tablespoons lime juice
1 tablespoon vegetable oil
1 small jalapeño chile, seeded and chopped (optional)
Salt and pepper to taste

Snapper
1 1/2 cups crushed potato chips
1/4 cup (1 ounce) grated Parmesan cheese
1 teaspoon thyme
1 pound red snapper, tilapia or catfish fillets,
cut into 1-inch wide strips
1/4 cup milk

For the salsa, combine the banana, bell peppers, scallions, cilantro, brown sugar, lime juice, oil, jalapeño, salt and pepper in a bowl and mix well. Chill, covered, in the refrigerator for 3 hours.

For the fish, preheat the oven to 475 degrees. Combine the potato chips, cheese and thyme in a bowl or sealable plastic bag. Dip the fish strips in the milk. Add the fish strips to the potato chip mixture, a few at a time, tossing to coat. Arrange the fish strips on a greased baking sheet. Bake for 8 to 10 minutes, turning once. Serve the fish with the salsa.

Serves 4

Snapper with Creamy Citrus Sauce

Sauce
4 shallots, thinly sliced
2 garlic cloves, chopped
2 tablespoons olive oil
1 (8-ounce) bottle clam juice
3/4 cup cream or heavy cream
1/2 cup white wine
1/2 cup fresh orange juice
2 tablespoons diced oil-pack sun-dried tomatoes
1 tablespoon fresh lime juice
1 teaspoon herbes de Provence
1 teaspoon Worcestershire sauce
1/2 teaspoon grated orange zest
1/2 teaspoon grated lime zest

Fish
4 (5- to 6-ounce) red snapper fillets
Salt and pepper to taste
All-purpose flour for dredging
2 tablespoons olive oil
8 ounces angel hair pasta
2 tablespoons chopped fresh basil leaves
Finely minced orange zest

For the sauce, sauté the shallots and garlic in the olive oil in a heavy skillet over medium-high heat for 30 seconds. Add the clam juice, cream, wine, orange juice, tomatoes, lime juice, herbes de Provence, Worcestershire sauce, grated orange and lime zest. Bring to a boil. Reduce the heat and simmer for 10 minutes or until reduced to 1 1/2 cups, stirring occasionally.

For the fish, season the fillets with salt and pepper. Place the flour in a shallow dish. Dredge the fish in the flour, coating both sides. Shake off the excess flour. Cook the fish in the olive oil in a large heavy skillet over medium heat for 4 minutes per side or until brown and the fish flakes easily, turning once. Remove the fish to a platter and keep warm. Pour the sauce into the skillet and bring to a simmer. Cook the pasta al dente using the package directions; drain. Return the pasta to the pot and add half the sauce; mix well. Divide the pasta among 4 individual serving plates. Top each with a fish fillet. Drizzle with the remaining sauce. Top with the basil and minced orange zest.

Serves 4

Grilled Swordfish with Avocado Mayonnaise

Fish
1 cup thinly sliced green onions
3/4 cup packed fresh cilantro leaves
1 1/2 tablespoons light brown sugar
1 1/2 tablespoons grated lime zest
3 tablespoons fresh lime juice
3 tablespoons olive oil
1 tablespoon coarsely chopped seeded jalapeño chile
Salt and pepper to taste
6 (8-ounce) swordfish steaks, each about 3/4 inch thick

Avocado Mayonnaise
2 large avocados, pitted and quartered
5 tablespoons mayonnaise
1 tablespoon fresh lime juice
3/4 teaspoon hot pepper sauce
Salt and pepper to taste

For the fish, combine the green onions, cilantro, brown sugar, lime zest, lime juice, olive oil and jalapeño in a food processor and process until almost smooth. Season with salt and pepper. Pour the green onion mixture into a 9×13-inch baking dish. Add the fish, turning to coat. Marinate, covered, in the refrigerator for 2 hours, turning the fish occasionally. Remove the fish from the marinade. Coat the grill rack with vegetable oil. Preheat the grill to medium. Grill for about 4 minutes per side or until the fish is opaque, turning once and basting frequently with the marinade. Remove the fish to a serving platter and top each with a dollop of avocado mayonnaise.

For the mayonnaise, combine the avocados, mayonnaise, lime juice and hot sauce in a blender and process until smooth. Season with salt and pepper.

Serves 6

Tilapia with Capers and Almonds

3/4 cup all-purpose flour
Salt and freshly ground pepper to taste
1 1/2 pounds tilapia, sole or
flounder fillets
3 tablespoons butter

2 teaspoons olive oil
1/4 cup slivered almonds
1/4 cup drained capers
1 lemon, sliced paper thin

Combine the flour, salt and pepper in a sealable plastic bag. Add the fish, a few pieces at a time, and shake to coat. Shake off the excess flour. Melt 1 tablespoon of the butter with 1 teaspoon of the olive oil in a large skillet over medium heat. Add half the fish and cook for 3 to 4 minutes or until golden brown and crisp, turning once. Remove to a platter and keep warm. Repeat the cooking process with 1 tablespoon butter, the remaining olive oil and remaining fish. Remove to the platter. Add the remaining 1 tablespoon butter and the almonds to the skillet. Cook for 2 minutes or until the almonds are golden brown. Add the capers and lemon slices and cook for 1 minute or until heated through. Pour the sauce over the fish and serve immediately.

Serves 4

Tuna Steaks with Basil Marinade

1 1/2 cups torn fresh basil leaves
1/2 cup olive oil
1/2 cup fresh lime juice
1 teaspoon chopped green onion
1/2 teaspoon grated lime zest
1/8 teaspoon salt

6 tuna steaks
2 avocados, peeled and diced
2 tomatoes, seeded and diced
5 teaspoons chopped green onion
Dash of Tabasco sauce

Combine the basil, olive oil, lime juice, 1 teaspoon green onion, lime zest and salt in a food processor. Pulse until the basil is chopped. Remove and reserve 3 tablespoons of the basil mixture. Arrange the tuna in a shallow baking dish and pour the remaining basil mixture over the tuna. Marinate, covered, in the refrigerator for at least 30 minutes, turning the tuna once.

Combine the avocados, tomatoes, 5 teaspoons green onion, the reserved basil mixture and Tabasco sauce in a bowl and mix well. Coat a grill rack with vegetable oil and preheat the grill. Grill the tuna over hot coals in an open grill for 3 to 4 minutes for rare, turning after 2 minutes and basting occasionally with the marinade. Serve the tuna with the avocado salsa.

Serves 6

Tuna with Wasabi Butter

Wasabi Butter
2 tablespoons wasabi powder
1 tablespoon fresh orange juice
$^1/_2$ cup (1 stick) unsalted butter, softened
1 tablespoon minced fresh cilantro
1 teaspoon kosher salt

Tuna
$^1/_3$ cup rice vinegar
3 tablespoons sugar
3 tablespoons dry sherry
2 tablespoons soy sauce
1 tablespoon chili garlic sauce
1 tablespoon sesame oil
$^1/_4$ cup chopped scallions
4 garlic cloves, crushed
4 thin slices fresh ginger, crushed
4 tuna steaks

For the butter, stir together the wasabi powder and orange juice in a bowl until smooth. Add the butter, cilantro and salt and mix well. Spread the mixture onto a sheet of plastic wrap and roll tightly into a log, twisting the ends of the plastic wrap to seal. Chill in the refrigerator until firm. Unwrap and slice into rounds.

For the tuna, whisk together the vinegar, sugar, sherry, soy sauce, chili garlic sauce and sesame oil in a bowl until blended. Stir in the scallions, garlic and ginger. Pour into a large sealable plastic bag and add the tuna steaks. Marinate, covered, in the refrigerator for 20 minutes. Coat a grill rack with vegetable oil. Preheat the grill to medium high. Remove the steaks from the marinade, discarding the marinade. Grill for 3 minutes per side for medium-rare or to desired doneness, turning once. Top with wasabi butter.

Serves 4

Meats & Poultry

Present sensational entrées,

savory sauces, and family favorites

with a fresh new twist.

Garlic Herb-Crusted Strip Loin Roast

4 garlic cloves
8 fresh sage leaves
4 teaspoons fresh thyme leaves
4 teaspoons coarse salt
4 teaspoons olive oil
1¹/₂ teaspoons pepper
1 (4- to 5-pound) boneless beef strip loin roast,
fat trimmed to ¹/₄ inch and roast rolled and tied

Turn on a food processor and add the garlic; process until finely chopped. Add the sage, thyme, salt, olive oil and pepper and process until a paste forms. Pat the meat dry with paper towels. Rub the herb paste all over the meat. Chill, covered, in the refrigerator for at least 3 hours or up to 1 day. Preheat the oven to 450 degrees. Place the meat fat side up on a rack in a large roasting pan. Roast for 15 minutes. Reduce the oven temperature to 350 degrees. Roast for about 35 minutes for medium-rare or until a meat thermometer inserted in the thickest part of the meat reads 130 degrees or to the desired degree of doneness. Remove to a cutting board and let rest for 20 minutes. Cut crosswise into ¹/₃-inch-thick slices and arrange on a serving platter.

Serves 10

Oven-Roasted Beef Brisket

1 tablespoon garlic powder
1 tablespoon seasoned salt
1 (3- to 4-pound) beef brisket
1 package onion soup mix
1 (12-ounce) can cola (not diet)
3 to 4 tablespoons ketchup

Preheat the oven to 425 degrees. Rub the garlic powder and seasoned salt all over the meat. Place the meat fat side up in a large roasting pan. Roast, uncovered, for 1 hour. Reduce the oven temperature to 325 degrees. Remove the meat from the oven and sprinkle with the onion soup mix. Pour the cola over the meat and spread with the ketchup. Cover the pan tightly with foil. Roast for 3 to 4 hours. Remove the meat to a cutting board and cut diagonally across the grain into thin slices. Serve immediately.

Note: The roasted brisket can be cooled in the pan then chilled in the refrigerator overnight. Skim off the fat, slice, and reheat.

Serves 6 to 8

Grilled Flank Steak

1 (2-pound) flank steak
Salt and pepper to taste
2 large shallots, chopped
2 tablespoons sugar
3 tablespoons balsamic vinegar
2 tablespoons soy sauce

Pat the steak dry with paper towels. Cut crosswise into 2 pieces. Season with salt and pepper and place in a large sealable plastic bag. Whisk together the shallots, sugar, vinegar and soy sauce in a small bowl until combined. Pour over the steak. Marinate in the refrigerator for at least 2 hours, turning the bag several times. Preheat the grill. Grill the steak over hot coals for 7 to 9 minutes for medium-rare. Remove to a cutting board and let stand, covered, for 10 minutes. Cut the steak diagonally across the grain into thin slices. Serve with sautéed mushrooms, if desired.

Serves 4 to 5

BEEF TENDERLOIN

*Nothing says special occasion like a beef tenderloin cooked to perfection.
By trying out a new cooking method or adding a special glaze or sauce, you can
completely change the feel of your meal. Follow our guide to the perfectly cooked
tenderloin and the perfect sauce to match.*

YOU WILL NEED:

4 to 5 pounds beef tenderloin, trimmed of excess fat and silver skin
Olive oil
Kosher salt
Freshly ground pepper
Let the meat stand at room temperature for 20 to 30 minutes before cooking.

ROASTING METHOD

Preheat the oven to 450 degrees. Rub the tenderloin with olive oil and season with salt and pepper. Bake in a shallow roasting pan for 35 minutes or until the internal temperature is 120 to 125 degrees on a meat thermometer for rare. Let the meat stand for 10 minutes before carving. The meat temperature will rise 5 to 10 degrees while resting.

WESTERN METHOD

Preheat the oven to 500 degrees. Season the tenderloin with salt and pepper and place in a shallow roasting pan. Place in the oven for exactly 5 minutes. Turn off the oven; do not open the door at any time! Leave in the oven for 1 hour. This will cook a 4-pound tenderloin to medium and a 5-pound tenderloin to medium-rare. Let the meat stand before carving.

GRILLING METHOD

Preheat the grill to medium. Rub the tenderloin with olive oil and season with salt and pepper. Sear over direct heat, turning a quarter turn every 5 minutes for a total of 20 minutes. Continue grilling over indirect heat for another 15 to 20 minutes for medium. Let the meat stand before carving.

Bourbon Glaze

1/4 cup bourbon   *1/4 cup packed light brown sugar*
1/4 cup Dijon mustard

Whisk the bourbon, Dijon mustard and brown sugar in a small bowl until well blended. Baste the tenderloin with the mixture during the last 10 minutes of grilling.

Peppercorn Rub

1 cup chopped parsley   *2 tablespoons green peppercorns*
1/4 cup (1/2 stick) butter, softened   *2 tablespoons red peppercorns*
3 tablespoons Dijon mustard

Mix the parsley, butter and Dijon mustard in a small bowl. Rub the mixture over the tenderloin and coat with the peppercorns. Chill, covered, in the refrigerator overnight. Remove from the refrigerator and bring to room temperature. Roast or grill to desired doneness.

Burgundy Sauce

1 cup burgundy   *3/4 cup butter*
1/4 cup soy sauce   *1 teaspoon lemon pepper*

Combine the wine, soy sauce, butter and lemon pepper in a small saucepan over medium heat until the butter is melted and the mixture is thoroughly heated, stirring constantly. Pour the sauce over the tenderloin 10 minutes into the roasting time. Continue to baste occasionally for the remaining cooking time.

Gorgonzola Sauce

4 cups cream or heavy cream   *3/4 teaspoon kosher salt*
3 to 4 ounces Gorgonzola cheese,   *3/4 teaspoon freshly ground pepper*
crumbled (not creamy or "dulce")   *3 tablespoons minced fresh parsley*
3 tablespoons freshly grated
Parmesan cheese

Bring the cream to a full boil in a medium saucepan over medium-high heat. Continue to boil rapidly for 45 to 50 minutes or until thickened like a white sauce, stirring frequently to make sure that the bottom does not burn. Remove from the heat and add the cheeses, salt, pepper and parsley. Whisk rapidly until the cheeses melt. Serve warm. If you must reheat the sauce, warm over low heat until melted, then whisk vigorously until the sauce comes together.

Beef with Broccoli

Beef Marinade
3 tablespoons soy sauce
2 tablespoons oyster sauce
1 tablespoon sugar
1 1/2 pounds boneless beef sirloin, cut across the grain into 1/4-inch-thick slices

Stir Fry
4 to 6 tablespoons vegetable oil
1/2 red onion, cut into wedges (optional)
1/2 red bell pepper, cut into strips (optional)
2 tablespoons minced peeled fresh ginger
2 tablespoons minced garlic
1 1/2 teaspoons red pepper flakes, or 1/2 to 1 teaspoon Oriental chili sauce

1 pound broccoli, separated into florets and stems chopped
1/3 cup water
8 ounces shiitake mushrooms or white mushrooms, sliced
Hot cooked rice

Stir-Fry Sauce
3 tablespoons cornstarch
2 tablespoons soy sauce
1 cup chicken broth, beef broth or water
1/4 cup dry sherry
1 tablespoon sugar
1 to 2 tablespoons sesame oil
Oriental chili sauce or chili paste to taste (optional)

For the marinade, stir together the soy sauce, oyster sauce and sugar in a bowl or sealable plastic bag. Add the beef. Marinate in the refrigerator for 20 minutes or longer. Remove the beef and set aside; discard the marinade.

For the stir fry, heat a wok or large heavy skillet over high heat and add 2 tablespoons of the oil. Heat just until it begins to smoke. Add the beef, onion and bell pepper in batches and stir-fry for 1 minute or until the meat is no longer pink. Remove with a slotted spoon to a platter.

Add 1 tablespoon of the oil to the wok and heat until hot. Add the ginger, garlic and red pepper flakes and stir-fry for 30 seconds or until fragrant. Add the broccoli and stir-fry for 1 minute. Add the water and steam the broccoli, covered, for 1 1/2 to 2 minutes or until tender-crisp. Add the mushrooms and stir-fry for 2 minutes.

For the sauce, whisk together the cornstarch and soy sauce in a bowl until blended. Whisk in the broth, sherry, sugar, sesame oil and chili sauce.

Add the sauce and beef mixture to the wok. Stir-fry for 2 minutes or until the sauce is thickened and the beef is heated through. Remove to a heated platter. Serve over the rice.

Note: Chicken or shrimp can be substituted for the beef.
Other vegetables can be added or substituted.

Serves 4 to 6

Braised Veal Roast Primavera

Veal Roast
1 (6- to 7-pound) boneless veal shoulder
roast, rolled and tied
Salt and pepper to taste
Olive oil

Primavera Sauce
1/2 cup chopped shallots
4 teaspoons minced garlic
1 cup white wine
2 cups chicken stock
1 cup diced seeded tomatoes
3 tablespoons chopped fresh basil leaves
1 tablespoon chopped fresh mint
1 tablespoon chopped fresh parsley
Grated zest of 1 lemon
1 teaspoon pepper
2 cups cream or heavy cream

Linguini
1 pound linguini
1 cup julienned arugula
1/4 cup (1/2 stick) butter
1/4 cup (1 ounce) grated Parmigiano-Reggiano cheese

For the roast, season the roast with salt and pepper. Coat the bottom of a Dutch oven or other large heavy pan with olive oil. Add the roast and brown well on all sides. Remove the roast from the pan.

For the sauce, sauté the shallots and garlic in the roast drippings until fragrant. Add the wine and stock and bring to boil, stirring to deglaze the pan and loosen the brown bits. Add the tomatoes, basil, mint, parsley, lemon zest and pepper. Add the roast to the sauce in the pan. Cook, tightly covered, for 3 hours or until the roast is very tender. Or roast, covered, in a 350-degree oven. Remove the roast from the pan to a cutting board and let stand, covered, for 10 minutes. Bring the sauce to a boil. Simmer until the sauce is reduced to 2 cups. Remove from the heat and stir in the cream. Cut the roast into 1 1/2- to 2-inch-thick slices and return to the pan with the sauce. Heat through.

For the linguini, cook the pasta using the package directions; drain. Return to the pot and stir in the arugula, butter and cheese.

To serve, place linguini mixture on individual serving plates and top each with a slice of meat and sauce.

Serves 8

Spinach- and Prosciutto-Stuffed Veal Chops

Stuffing
1/2 cup finely chopped yellow onion
1 tablespoon extra-virgin olive oil
2 teaspoons minced garlic
2 plum tomatoes, seeded and chopped
1 (10-ounce) package frozen chopped spinach, thawed and squeezed dry
3 slices prosciutto, finely chopped
1/2 cup (2 ounces) shredded fontina cheese
1/2 teaspoon kosher salt
1/4 teaspoon freshly ground pepper

Veal
4 (1 1/4- to 1 1/2-inch-thick) veal chops, trimmed
Olive oil
2 teaspoons finely chopped fresh rosemary leaves
1/2 teaspoon kosher salt
1/2 teaspoon freshly ground pepper

For the stuffing, sauté the onion in 1 tablespoon olive oil in a large skillet or sauté pan over medium heat for 5 to 6 minutes or until tender. Add the garlic and sauté for 1 minute. Add the tomatoes and cook for 2 minutes longer. Remove from the heat and cool for 3 to 4 minutes. Stir in the spinach, prosciutto, cheese, 1/2 teaspoon salt and 1/4 teaspoon pepper and mix well. Divide the mixture into 4 portions.

For the veal, cut a slit in the side of each chop and stuff the spinach mixture into each pocket. Close with wooden picks. Brush the chops lightly with additional olive oil. Stir together the rosemary, 1/2 teaspoon salt and 1/2 teaspoon pepper in a small bowl. Rub the rosemary mixture over the chops. Let stand at room temperature for 20 to 30 minutes. Coat a grill rack with vegetable oil, if desired. Preheat the grill. Grill the chops for 15 to 20 minutes for medium-rare, turning once after 10 minutes. Remove from the grill to a serving platter and let stand for 3 to 5 minutes before serving.

Serves 4

Veal Osso Buco with Gremolata

Veal

8 (12- to 14-ounce) crosscut veal shanks
2¹/4 teaspoons salt
1¹/4 teaspoons pepper
³/4 cup all-purpose flour
¹/4 cup (¹/2 stick) unsalted butter
2 tablespoons olive oil
¹/2 bay leaf
6 sprigs fresh parsley
4 sprigs fresh thyme
1 onion, chopped
2 carrots, chopped

2 ribs celery, chopped
1 garlic clove, minced
4 plum tomatoes, seeded and chopped
Dash of salt and pepper
1¹/2 cups dry white wine
2 to 3 cups chicken stock or beef stock

Gremolata

¹/4 cup minced fresh parsley
1 tablespoon grated lemon zest
1¹/2 teaspoons minced garlic

For the veal, pat the veal shanks dry with paper towels and season with 2¹/4 teaspoons salt and 1¹/4 teaspoons pepper. Dredge the veal shanks in the flour, shaking off the excess. Melt 1 tablespoon of the butter with 1 tablespoon of the olive oil in a large heavy ovenproof skillet or Dutch oven. Add 4 veal shanks and brown on all sides. Remove to a platter. Add 1 tablespoon of the butter and remaining 1 tablespoon olive oil to the skillet and brown the remaining 4 veal shanks on all sides. Remove to the platter. Wipe the skillet.

Preheat the oven to 325 degrees. Wrap the bay leaf, parsley and thyme in a piece of cheesecloth and tie to make a bouquet garni. Melt the remaining 2 tablespoons butter in the skillet. Add the onion, carrots, celery and garlic and cook for 8 minutes or until tender. Stir in the tomatoes and bouquet garni. Season with a dash of salt and pepper.

Return the veal to the skillet and add the wine and enough stock to almost cover the veal. Bring to a boil. Cover the skillet and place in the oven. Bake for 2 to 2¹/2 hours or until the veal is fork tender.

Remove the veal from the skillet. Skim off any fat and strain the mixture. Return the liquid to the skillet and bring to a boil. Return the veal to the skillet, spooning the liquid over the veal. Return to the oven and bake uncovered for 15 minutes to glaze the veal.

For the gremolata, stir together the parsley, lemon zest and garlic. Sprinkle over the shanks before serving.

Serves 6 to 8

Lamb Ragu

¹/₃ cup minced yellow onion
¹/₃ cup minced carrots
¹/₃ cup minced celery
¹/₃ cup extra-virgin olive oil
1 pound lamb shoulder, chopped
1 cup dry white wine
3 cups canned Italian plum tomatoes and juice
1¹/₂ cups chicken broth
Salt and freshly ground pepper to taste
1 cup shelled fresh peas, or frozen green peas, thawed
2 to 3 tablespoons cream or heavy cream
1 cup (4 ounces) freshly grated Parmigiano-Reggiano cheese

Sauté the onion, carrots and celery in the olive oil in a large heavy skillet or saucepan over medium heat for 7 to 8 minutes or until the vegetables are tender and golden brown. Increase the heat to high and add the lamb. Cook for 3 to 4 minutes or until the lamb is no longer pink, stirring frequently. Add the wine and cook for 2 to 3 minutes or until it has almost entirely evaporated.

Press the tomatoes through a food mill to remove the seeds. Add the tomatoes and broth to the skillet. Season with salt and pepper. Bring to a boil. Reduce the heat to low and partially cover the skillet. Simmer for 30 to 35 minutes or until thickened, stirring occasionally. Stir in the peas and cream and cook for 1 minute. Taste and adjust the seasonings. Sprinkle with the cheese just before serving. Serve with pasta or garlic mashed potatoes.

Note: If using frozen peas, add with the cream and heat through.

Serves 4 to 6

Pecan-Encrusted Lamb Chops

1/4 cup (1/2 stick) butter, melted
3/4 cup finely chopped pecans
1/4 cup fresh bread crumbs
2 tablespoons grated Parmesan cheese
2 tablespoons chopped fresh
rosemary leaves

2 teaspoons minced garlic
2 racks of lamb, cut into chops
(6 to 8 chops each)
Salt and pepper to taste
2 tablespoons peanut oil

Preheat the oven to 350 degrees. Combine the butter, pecans, bread crumbs, cheese, rosemary and garlic in a bowl and mix well. Press the pecan mixture onto both sides of the chops. Season with salt and pepper. Heat the peanut oil in a large skillet and brown the chops on both sides. Remove the chops to a shallow baking pan. Bake for 10 to 15 minutes for rare to medium-rare, or until a meat thermometer reads 120 to 125 degrees.

Serves 6

Marinated Pork Roast with Red Currant Sauce

Roast
1 tablespoon all-purpose flour
1 tablespoon dry mustard
1 teaspoon ground ginger
1 teaspoon dried thyme leaves, crushed
1 garlic clove, minced
1/2 cup soy sauce

1/2 cup orange juice
1 (3-pound) boneless pork loin roast,
rolled and tied

Red Currant Sauce
1 (10-ounce) jar red currant jelly
2 tablespoons orange juice
1 tablespoon soy sauce

For the pork roast, sprinkle the flour in a 14×20-inch oven cooking bag and shake well. Place the bag in a large deep roasting pan. Add the dry mustard, ginger, thyme, garlic, soy sauce and orange juice to the bag. Place the roast in the bag and close with the plastic fastener. Turn the bag gently several times to mix the ingredients and coat the meat. Marinate in the refrigerator overnight, turning the bag once or twice.

Preheat the oven to 325 degrees. Cook the roast in the bag using the package directions for 1 to 1 1/2 hours or until a meat thermometer inserted into the meat reads 160 degrees. Remove from the oven to a cutting board and let stand for 15 minutes before slicing.

For the sauce, combine the jelly, orange juice and soy sauce in a saucepan and bring to a boil. Reduce the heat and simmer for 2 minutes. Pour into a serving dish. Serve with the pork roast.

Serves 6

Pork Tenderloin with Island Sauce

2 (³/4- to 1-pound) pork
tenderloins, trimmed
3 tablespoons orange juice
1¹/2 tablespoons Jamaican jerk seasoning
¹/2 cup red currant jelly

¹/4 cup Dijon mustard
1¹/2 tablespoons dark rum
¹/4 cup fresh raspberries
¹/2 cup golden raisins (optional)
Chopped honey-roasted peanuts

Coat a grill rack with nonstick cooking spray. Preheat the grill to medium-high (350 to 400 degrees). Brush the tenderloins with the orange juice and rub with the jerk seasoning. Grill the tenderloins for 15 to 20 minutes or until a meat thermometer inserted in the meat reads 140 degrees, turning frequently. Remove the tenderloins to a cutting board and let stand, covered, for 5 to 10 minutes before slicing. Whisk together the jelly and Dijon mustard in a small saucepan. Cook over low heat until combined, stirring constantly. Remove from the heat and stir in the rum, raspberries and raisins. Drizzle the sauce over the sliced tenderloins and sprinkle with peanuts. Serve with long grain rice and wild rice, if desired.

Serves 4 to 6

Pork Medallions with Dried Cherries

1 cup ruby port or
sweet vermouth
¹/3 cup dried sweet cherries
4 teaspoons seedless raspberry jam
1 teaspoon Dijon mustard
1 tablespoon vegetable oil

1¹/2 pounds pork tenderloin, trimmed
and cut into 16 slices
¹/2 teaspoon salt
¹/4 teaspoon freshly ground pepper
1 tablespoon butter
Fresh parsley sprigs for garnish

Combine the wine, dried cherries, jam and Dijon mustard in a small bowl and mix well. Heat the oil in a large nonstick skillet over low heat for 2 minutes. Season the pork with the salt and pepper. Place the pork in the hot skillet and cook for 4 minutes, without turning, until golden brown. Turn the pork and cook for 4 minutes, without turning, until golden brown. Remove the pork to a platter and keep warm. Add the cherry mixture to the skillet, stirring to deglaze the pan and loosen the brown bits. Bring to a boil over high heat and cook for 3 minutes or until the mixture is reduced to ¹/2 cup. Remove from the heat and whisk in the butter. Serve the sauce over the pork. Garnish with parsley.

Serves 4 to 6

Grilled Pork Tenderloin

2 (³/4- to 1-pound) pork tenderloins, trimmed
¹/4 cup soy sauce
1¹/2 tablespoons honey
2 tablespoons sake or dry sherry
1 tablespoon grated fresh ginger
2 garlic cloves, minced
1 tablespoon butter
Salt and pepper to taste

Fold the narrow ends of the tenderloins under to make the meat a uniform thickness; tie with kitchen string. Combine the soy sauce, honey, sake, ginger and garlic in a large sealable plastic bag. Add the tenderloins to the bag. Marinate in the refrigerator for at least 30 minutes or up to 1 day.

Remove the tenderloins from the marinade. Pour the marinade into a glass measuring cup and microwave on high for 1 minute. Coat a grill rack with vegetable oil. Preheat the grill to medium. Grill the tenderloins, 4 to 6 inches from the coals, for 15 to 20 minutes or until a meat thermometer inserted in the meat reads 140 degrees, turning frequently and brushing with the marinade.

Remove the tenderloins to a cutting board and let stand for 5 minutes before slicing. Slice the tenderloins.

Note: Serve the Grilled Pork Tenderloin with Golden Curried Couscous (page 118)
and steamed pea pods for a delicious, healthy meal.

Serves 4 to 6

Chicken with Artichokes

1 (12-ounce) jar marinated artichoke
  hearts, drained and marinade reserved
4 boneless skinless chicken breasts,
  pounded to 1/4-inch thickness
Salt and pepper to taste
1 to 2 tablespoons olive oil (optional)
8 ounces button mushrooms, sliced
1 (14-ounce) can chicken broth

1/2 cup white wine
2 tablespoons Dijon mustard
3 Roma tomatoes, seeded and diced
2 teaspoons cornstarch
2 tablespoons cold water
1/4 cup chopped fresh basil leaves
  for garnish

Pour the reserved artichoke marinade into a large skillet or sauté pan and heat over medium-high heat. Season the chicken with salt and pepper. Sauté the chicken in the marinade for 3 to 4 minutes or until light brown and the chicken is no longer pink. Remove the chicken to a platter and keep warm. Add the olive oil to the skillet if needed. Add the mushrooms and sauté until tender. Stir in the broth, wine and Dijon mustard. Add the artichoke hearts and tomatoes. Stir together the cornstarch and water in a small bowl until blended. Stir the cornstarch mixture into the sauce and bring to a boil. Return the chicken to the skillet and heat through, spooning the sauce over the chicken. Serve the chicken with the sauce and garnish with the basil.

Serves 4

Chicken with Marsala Sage Sauce

4 boneless skinless chicken breasts,
  each sliced horizontally in half
Salt and pepper to taste
All-purpose flour
6 tablespoons butter

1 tablespoon chopped fresh sage
1 cup dry marsala
1 cup low-salt chicken broth
Fresh sage leaves for garnish

Season the chicken with salt and pepper. Dredge in flour, shaking off the excess. Melt 3 tablespoons of the butter in a large skillet over medium-high heat. Add the chopped sage and sauté for 1 minute. Add half the chicken. Sauté for 3 minutes, without turning, until brown. Turn and sauté for 3 minutes or until brown and chicken is no longer pink. Remove the chicken to a platter and keep warm. Repeat the process with the remaining butter and chicken. Remove to the platter. Add the marsala and broth to the skillet and bring to a boil, stirring to deglaze the pan and loosen any brown bits. Cook for about 10 minutes or until the sauce is reduced to 1/2 cup. Season with salt and pepper. Spoon the sauce over the chicken to serve. Garnish with sage leaves.

Serves 4

Crispy Chicken with Maple Vinegar Sauce

Topping
2¹/2 tablespoons butter
³/4 cup slivered almonds
¹/2 cup dried cranberries
¹/2 cup thinly sliced leek
1¹/2 tablespoons dry bread crumbs
Kosher salt and freshly ground
pepper to taste

Maple Vinegar Sauce
2 tablespoons butter
¹/4 cup chopped shallots
¹/2 teaspoon pepper
¹/2 cup cider vinegar
¹/2 cup maple syrup

Chicken
1 (4-pound) chicken, cut into pieces
1¹/2 tablespoons kosher salt
Freshly ground pepper
3 tablespoons vegetable oil

For the topping, melt the butter in a small skillet and add the almonds. Toast until golden brown, stirring frequently. Add the dried cranberries and leek and cook for 1 minute. Stir in the bread crumbs and season with salt and pepper.

For the sauce, melt the butter in a saucepan or skillet. Add the shallots and sauté until translucent. Add the pepper and vinegar and bring to a boil. Add the maple syrup and simmer until reduced by half or to the desired consistency.

For the chicken, preheat the oven to 500 degrees. Season the chicken with the salt and pepper. Heat the oil in a large ovenproof skillet or Dutch oven. Add the chicken, a few pieces at a time, and cook until brown and crispy, turning frequently. Return all the chicken to the skillet. Bake for about 25 minutes or until the chicken is no longer pink. Remove the chicken to a platter and keep warm. Skim off the fat, reserving the drippings in the skillet. Add the maple vinegar sauce and bring to a boil. Cook for 1 minute, stirring to deglaze the pan and loosen the brown bits. Sprinkle the chicken with the topping and drizzle with the warm sauce. Serve any remaining sauce on the side.

Serves 8 to 10

TRENDY NEW RECIPES, SUCH AS CRISPY CHICKEN WITH MAPLE vinegar sauce, are just a few of the things Marist alumni Daniel O'Brien is mastering at the Culinary Institute of America. A member of the Marist class of 1999, the talented young Atlanta chef received an associate degree in culinary arts before his current studies in the Culinary Institute's Hospitality Management Program. In addition to the time spent in the classroom, O'Brien has gained invaluable experience from his work as a sous chef at the upscale Italian restaurant, Caterina di Medici.

Caribbean Chicken

2 tablespoons whole allspice
1 teaspoon ground cinnamon
1 teaspoon nutmeg
1 large onion, chopped
2 cups sliced green onions
1 cup olive oil
1 cup fresh orange juice
1/4 cup fresh lime juice
1/4 cup soy sauce

1/4 cup red wine vinegar
2 tablespoons minced peeled fresh ginger
3 garlic cloves
1 or 2 Scotch bonnet chiles or habanero
   chiles, seeded and chopped
1 teaspoon salt
1 cup barbecue sauce
6 to 8 chicken breasts
Salt and pepper to taste

Combine the allspice, cinnamon and nutmeg in a small skillet over medium heat. Heat for 1 minute or until fragrant, stirring constantly. Finely grind the spice mixture in a spice grinder. Place the spice mixture, chopped onion, green onions, olive oil, orange juice, lime juice, soy sauce, vinegar, ginger, garlic, chiles and 1 teaspoon salt in a food processor and process until smooth. Combine 1 1/2 cups of the puréed mixture with the barbecue sauce in a bowl or jar. Store, covered, in the refrigerator. Place the chicken in a 9×13-inch baking dish or large sealable plastic bag. Pour the remaining puréed mixture over the chicken, turning the chicken to coat. Marinate, covered, in the refrigerator overnight. Preheat the grill to medium. Remove the chicken from the marinade; discard the marinade. Season the chicken with salt and pepper. Grill until the chicken is no longer pink, turning frequently. Pour the reserved barbecue sauce mixture into a saucepan. Bring to a boil. Reduce the heat and simmer for 5 minutes. Serve the sauce with the chicken.

Serves 6 to 8

Mediterranean Chicken

1/2 cup olive oil
1/3 cup balsamic vinegar
1 onion, chopped
6 garlic cloves, minced
1 (14-ounce) can diced tomatoes with
   Italian seasonings, drained
1/2 cup chopped kalamata
   olives (optional)

2 tablespoons chopped fresh parsley
1 tablespoon chopped fresh oregano, or
   1 teaspoon dried oregano
1/8 teaspoon crushed red pepper flakes
   (optional)
Salt and pepper to taste
4 to 6 boneless skinless chicken breasts

Preheat the oven to 350 degrees. Mix the olive oil, vinegar, onion, garlic, tomatoes, olives, parsley, oregano, red pepper flakes, salt and pepper in a bowl. Place the chicken in a shallow baking dish and pour the tomato mixture over the top. Bake for 35 minutes or until the chicken is no longer pink. Serve with rice.

Serves 4 to 6

Puttanesca Chicken

1/4 cup Italian-seasoned dry
 bread crumbs
1/2 teaspoon basil
1/2 teaspoon oregano
1/2 teaspoon salt
1/2 teaspoon freshly ground pepper
4 boneless skinless chicken breasts
3 tablespoons olive oil
2 cups sliced Vidalia onions

2 garlic cloves, minced
6 ounces (3/4 cup) beer
3 tablespoons chopped kalamata olives
1 (15-ounce) can diced tomatoes,
 drained
Freshly grated Parmesan cheese or
 Romano cheese
Fresh mixed greens, rice or pasta

Combine the bread crumbs, basil, oregano, salt and pepper in a large sealable plastic bag and shake well. Add the chicken and shake well to coat. Heat the olive oil in a large skillet over medium heat. Add the chicken and sauté for 4 minutes or until brown. Turn the chicken over and sauté for 4 minutes or until brown. Remove the chicken to a platter and keep warm. Add the onions and garlic to the skillet and sauté until tender. Add the beer and olives and return the chicken to the pan. Cook for 5 to 10 minutes or until most of the liquid has evaporated, turning the chicken frequently. Add the tomatoes during the last 5 minutes of cooking. Sprinkle with cheese before serving. Serve over greens, rice or pasta.

Serves 4

Chicken Curry

2 tablespoons olive oil
6 carrots, diced
2 onions, sliced
6 ribs celery, diced
Vegetable oil
Salt and pepper to taste

1/2 teaspoon mild curry powder, or to taste
6 boneless skinless chicken breasts, each
 cut into 3 pieces
1 to 2 cups chicken broth
1/2 to 1 cup cream or heavy cream
Hot cooked basmati rice or jasmine rice

Heat the olive oil in a large skillet. Add the carrots, onions and celery and sauté for 10 to 15 minutes or until tender and light brown. Remove to a bowl. Coat the bottom of the skillet with vegetable oil and heat over high heat. Sprinkle the salt, pepper and curry powder over the chicken. Sauté the chicken for 3 to 4 minutes, until brown. Turn the chicken over and sauté for 3 to 4 minutes, until brown. Return the vegetables to the skillet and add enough broth to cover. Cook over medium heat for 10 to 15 minutes. Season with salt, pepper and additional curry powder. Simmer for 10 minutes to reduce the liquid. Stir in the cream and simmer for 5 minutes longer or to desired consistency, stirring occasionally. Taste and adjust the seasonings. Serve over rice.

Serves 6 to 8

Cuban Chicken and Rice

1 (3-pound) chicken
Salt and black pepper to taste
2 tablespoons vegetable oil
1 cup chopped onion
1 red bell pepper, chopped
1 garlic clove, minced
1 cup uncooked arborio rice or brown rice
1 envelope con azafrán seasoning
Cayenne pepper to taste
1 (8-ounce) can tomato sauce
6 ounces (3/4 cup) beer

Place the chicken in a large pot and cover with water or chicken broth. Season with salt and pepper. Bring to a boil. Reduce the heat and cook the chicken for 30 to 45 minutes or until tender. Remove the chicken from the pot to a cutting board and cool. Strain and reserve 2 cups of the chicken stock.

Heat the oil in a Dutch oven or other large heavy pan. Add the onion, bell pepper and garlic and sauté until tender. Add the rice, 2 cups reserved broth, con azafrán seasoning, salt and cayenne pepper. Bring to a boil. Reduce the heat and simmer, covered, for 10 minutes. Remove the chicken from the bones in large pieces. Add the chicken, tomato sauce and beer to the rice mixture. Cook, covered, for 15 minutes longer or until the liquid is absorbed and the rice is tender.

Serves 4

Duck with Blackberry Sauce

Blackberry Sauce
2 tablespoons butter
3 tablespoons sugar
1/3 cup dry white wine
1/3 cup orange juice
2 tablespoons raspberry vinegar
1 1/4 cups fresh blackberries or frozen blackberries, thawed
1 1/4 cups beef broth
1/2 cup low-salt chicken broth
2 tablespoons cognac
1 tablespoon maple syrup
1 tablespoon butter
Salt and pepper to taste

Duck
4 boneless duck breasts
Salt and pepper to taste
Blackberries for garnish

For the sauce, melt 2 tablespoons butter in a large heavy nonstick skillet over medium-high heat. Add the sugar and cook for about 5 minutes or until caramelized to a deep amber color, stirring constantly. Stir in the wine, orange juice and vinegar and bring to a boil. Add the blackberries, beef broth and chicken broth. Cook for about 25 minutes or until thickened and reduced to about 1 cup, stirring occasionally. Strain the sauce through a sieve into a heavy saucepan, pressing with a spoon to purée the berries. Stir in the cognac and maple syrup. The sauce can be made ahead to this point. Store, covered, in the refrigerator. When ready to serve, bring the sauce to a simmer and whisk in 1 tablespoon butter until melted. Season with salt and pepper.

For the duck, score the skin in a crisscross pattern being careful not to cut into the flesh. Season with salt and pepper. Heat a large skillet or sauté pan over high heat. Place the duck skin side down in the hot pan. Reduce the heat to low and cook, covered with a splatter screen, for 10 minutes. Turn the duck over and cook for 2 minutes longer. Remove to a cutting board and let stand for 5 minutes before slicing.

To serve, spoon the sauce onto 4 individual serving plates. Slice the duck and arrange on top of the sauce. Garnish with blackberries. Serve with wild rice.

Serves 4

Side Dishes

Roast, mash, steam, or

grill to create interesting sides

with fabulous flavors.

Vegetable Napoleons

Roasted Vegetables
1/2 cup olive oil

1 pound unpeeled eggplant, cut
crosswise into twelve 1/3-inch slices

1 1/4 pounds unpeeled zucchini,cut
crosswise into twenty-four
1/3-inch slices

4 large plum tomatoes
(about 1 1/4 pounds), cut into
twelve to eighteen 1/3-inch slices

2 red onions, cut into
twelve 1/3-inch slices

1 pound unpeeled red potatoes,
cut into twelve 1/3-inch slices

Salt and pepper to taste

Filling
3/4 cup ricotta cheese

1 egg

2 tablespoons grated Parmesan cheese

1 tablespoon chopped fresh parsley

1 1/2 teaspoons chopped fresh
thyme leaves

Salt and pepper

Assembly
8 ounces mozzarella cheese, cut into six
1/4-inch slices

6 fresh rosemary sprigs

For the vegetables, position the oven racks in the middle and lower third of the oven. Preheat the oven to 450 degrees. Brush 2 large baking sheets with some of the olive oil. Arrange slices of the eggplant, zucchini, tomatoes, onions and potatoes in a single layer on the baking sheets. Brush with some of the olive oil and season with salt and pepper. Roast the vegetables for 10 to 15 minutes or until tender and light brown, switching the positions of the baking sheets after 5 minutes. Remove the vegetables to a large tray and arrange in a single layer. Repeat the roasting using the remaining vegetables and olive oil. The vegetables can be roasted 1 day ahead. Cool completely, layered between sheets of plastic wrap on large trays. Chill, covered, in the refrigerator. Bring to room temperature before proceeding.

For the filling, combine the ricotta cheese, egg, Parmesan cheese, parsley, thyme, salt and pepper in a bowl and mix well.

To assemble, preheat the oven to 450 degrees. Place 1 eggplant slice on a lightly oiled baking sheet. Spread with 1 tablespoon of the filling. Layer with 2 potato slices, 2 zucchini slices, 1 onion slice, 1 mozzarella slice, 2 or 3 tomato slices, 2 zucchini slices and 1 onion slice. Spread with 1 tablespoon filling and top with 1 eggplant slice. Repeat layering with the remaining vegetables and filling to make 5 more napoleons. Insert a skewer through the center of each napoleon to make a hole from top to bottom. Trim the rosemary sprigs to 1 inch taller than the napoleons. Remove the bottom leaves from the sprigs, leaving about 1 inch of leaves on the tops. Insert 1 rosemary sprig into each napoleon. Bake for 5 minutes or until the mozzarella is melted and the vegetables are heated through.

Serves 6

Chilled Vegetable Terrine

2 tablespoons olive oil
2 zucchini, cut into 1/4-inch slices
1 red onion, halved lengthwise and sliced
1 teaspoon minced garlic
Kosher salt and pepper to taste
2 red bell peppers, halved, cored and seeded
2 yellow bell peppers, halved, cored and seeded
1 unpeeled eggplant, cut into 1/4-inch slices
2 tablespoons olive oil
1/2 cup (2 ounces) grated Parmesan cheese
Red Pepper Coulis (below)

Preheat the oven to 400 degrees. Heat 2 tablespoons oil in a large sauté pan or skillet. Add the zucchini, onion and garlic and sauté for 10 minutes. Season with salt and pepper.

Arrange the bell peppers and eggplant slices on a baking sheet and brush with 2 tablespoons olive oil and season with salt and pepper. Roast for 30 to 40 minutes. Remove from the oven and cool.

Arrange half the eggplant slices in a single overlapping layer over the bottom of a 6-inch round baking pan (do not use a different size pan). Sprinkle with some of the Parmesan cheese and season with salt and pepper. Layer half the zucchini mixture, all of the red bell peppers, all of the yellow bell peppers and the remaining zucchini mixture, sprinkling with the Parmesan cheese and seasoning with the salt and pepper between each layer. Top with the remaining eggplant slices. Cover with waxed paper.

Place a flat 6-inch plate over the waxed paper and top with a heavy can or jar to compress the mixture. Chill in the refrigerator for 1 to 3 hours. Remove the can or jar. Let the terrine come to room temperature. Drain off the liquid. Invert the terrine onto a glass pedestal cake stand. Garnish with fresh greens or roasted grape tomatoes. Drizzle with Red Pepper Coulis before serving.

Note: Six-inch cake pans can be found at craft stores in the specialty baking section.

Serves 8

RED PEPPER COULIS

Combine 12 ounces roasted red peppers, 1 minced clove garlic, 1 tablespoon chopped fresh basil leaves, the juice of 1 lemon, 1 tablespoon olive oil and a pinch of red pepper flakes in a blender or food processor. Process until smooth. Season with salt and pepper to taste.

Roasted Root Vegetables with Herb Vinaigrette

Roasted Vegetables

6 tablespoons extra-virgin olive oil
2¹/₂ tablespoons chopped fresh
thyme leaves
2¹/₂ tablespoons chopped fresh marjoram
2 pounds sweet potatoes, peeled, halved lengthwise and
cut into 1¹/₄-inch slices
1¹/₂ pounds carrots, peeled and
cut into ³/₄-inch slices (about 4 cups)
1¹/₂ pounds parsnips, peeled and
cut into ³/₄-inch slices (about 4 cups)
1¹/₂ pounds rutabagas, peeled and cut into
¹/₂-inch pieces (about 4 cups)
2 red onions, root ends intact and cut into ¹/₂-inch wedges
Salt and pepper

Herb Vinaigrette

3 tablespoons extra-virgin olive oil
3 tablespoons balsamic vinegar
3 tablespoons chopped fresh parsley
2 teaspoons grated lemon zest
Fresh parsley sprigs for garnish

For the vegetables, position 1 oven rack in the top third of the oven and 1 rack in the bottom third and preheat the oven to 425 degrees. Whisk together the olive oil, thyme and marjoram in a large bowl. Add the sweet potatoes, carrots, parsnips, rutabagas and onions and toss to coat. Season generously with salt and pepper. Divide the vegetables between 2 large rimmed baking sheets coated with nonstick cooking spray. Roast for about 50 minutes or until tender and light brown, turning occasionally. The vegetables can be roasted 4 hours ahead. Let stand at room temperature. Warm in a 350-degree oven for 15 minutes, if desired. Vegetables can be served hot or at room temperature.

For the vinaigrette, whisk together the olive oil, vinegar, parsley and lemon zest in a small bowl until blended. Drizzle over the warm, roasted vegetables just before serving. Garnish with parsley sprigs.

Serves 8 to 10

Spring Vegetable Medley

6 ounces carrots, peeled
6 ounces green beans, trimmed
6 ounces asparagus, trimmed
6 ounces sugar snap peas
1 1/2 tablespoons salt
1/2 small red onion, chopped

2 tablespoons olive oil
6 ounces cherry tomatoes, halved
Salt to taste
1/8 teaspoon pepper
1/2 cup fresh basil leaves, torn in half

Cut the carrots, green beans, asparagus and snap peas diagonally into 1-inch pieces; set aside. Bring a large pot of water to a boil and add 1 1/2 tablespoons salt and the carrots. Blanch for 2 minutes. Add the green beans, asparagus and sugar snap peas and blanch for 2 minutes. Drain and immediately immerse the vegetables in ice water to stop the cooking process. Drain on paper towels. Sauté the onion in the olive oil in a large skillet over low heat for 3 to 4 minutes, stirring occasionally. Add the blanched vegetables and tomatoes and season with salt and pepper. Increase the heat to high and cook for 5 minutes, stirring occasionally. Remove from the heat. Add the basil and toss.

Serves 4

Seasonal Grilled Vegetables

Grilled Vegetables
1 eggplant, cut into 1/2-inch slices
3 sweet onions, cut into
1/2-inch semicircles
3 bell peppers (mixture of red,
green, yellow or orange)
3 yellow squash
3 zucchini
1 pound asparagus
1/4 cup olive oil
Salt and pepper

Balsamic Vinaigrette
2 tablespoons olive oil
3 tablespoons balsamic vinegar
1 teaspoon chopped fresh Italian parsley
1 teaspoon chopped fresh basil
1/2 teaspoon chopped fresh rosemary

For the vegetables, arrange the eggplant and onions on a baking sheet. Cut the bell peppers, squash, zucchini and asparagus into 1/2-inch strips and arrange on a separate baking sheet. Brush the vegetables with the olive oil and sprinkle with salt and pepper.

Working in batches, grill the vegetables over hot coals for 4 to 8 minutes per side or until tender. Remove to a serving platter.

For the vinaigrette, whisk the olive oil, vinegar, parsley, basil and rosemary in a small bowl until blended. Pour the mixture over the warm vegetables.

Serve warm or chilled.

Serves 6 to 8

Green Bean Bundles

2 pounds whole fresh
green beans, trimmed
8 ounces bacon, slices cut in half
1/4 cup (1/2 stick) butter or margarine
3 tablespoons brown sugar
Garlic salt to taste

Preheat the oven to 350 degrees. Blanch the green beans in a large pot of boiling water for 10 minutes. Drain in a colander and immediately rinse under cold running water until cool. Drain on paper towels. Gather 8 to 10 beans into a bundle and wrap with a half slice of bacon. Secure with a wooden pick. Repeat to use all the green beans. Arrange the bundles in a greased shallow baking dish. Combine the butter and brown sugar in a small saucepan over medium-low heat. Cook until the sugar dissolves, stirring occasionally. Pour the butter mixture over the bundles. Sprinkle with garlic salt. Bake for 30 to 40 minutes or until the bacon is cooked through.

Serves 8

Crunchy Broccoli Toss

1 1/2 pounds broccoli florets
4 garlic cloves, chopped
1/4 cup extra-virgin olive oil
2/3 cup panko (Japanese bread crumbs)
1/4 teaspoon each salt and pepper

Steam the broccoli for 8 to 10 minutes or until tender-crisp; drain. Sauté the garlic in the olive oil in a large skillet over medium heat for 5 minutes or until golden brown. Add the panko. Cook until golden brown, stirring constantly. Remove from the heat. Toss the broccoli and garlic mixture in a large bowl until combined. Serve immediately.

Variation: Use string beans instead of broccoli, add 1/2 teaspoon fresh lemon zest or
a sprinkle of Parmesan cheese and red pepper flakes.

Serves 4 to 6

Asparagus Spear Wraps

2 1/4 pounds fresh asparagus, trimmed   2 tablespoons lemon juice
3 yellow squash, cut into 1/2-inch slices   3/4 teaspoon fines herbes
1/4 cup (1/2 stick) butter   1 (2-ounce) jar sliced pimento, drained

Cook the asparagus in a large pot of boiling water, covered, for 6 to 8 minutes or until tender-crisp; drain. Steam the squash in a small amount of water in a saucepan for 3 minutes or until tender-crisp. Remove the seeds and center of each squash slice, leaving a 1/4-inch ring. Insert 4 to 6 asparagus spears into each squash ring. Arrange on a serving platter. Combine the butter, lemon juice and fines herbes in a small saucepan over low heat. Cook until the butter melts. Remove from the heat and stir in the pimentos. Drizzle the butter mixture over the asparagus wraps.

Serves 10

Presentation makes this dish ideal for entertaining, and the vegetable and sauce options are endless. The bundles can be prepared in advance and easily reheated in a 350-degree oven until warm. Do not drizzle with sauce until ready to serve.

- Instead of using just asparagus, do a medley of asparagus, julienned carrots and string beans, or use a single vegetable with a tarragon butter sauce.
- For the pepper lover, do a medley of red, green, and orange pepper strips bundled with zucchini strips. Simply microwave the vegetables until crisp before assembling. Finish on the grill on a vegetable grate. Drizzle with olive oil and sprinkle with freshly grated Romano cheese.
- Replace the yellow squash with zucchini, or use squash spears instead of the asparagus. Cook vegetables until crisp. Assemble and serve with a drizzle of Red Pepper Coulis (recipe featured with the Chilled Vegetable Terrine on page 105).
- Substitute the topping with hollandaise sauce to give the vegetables a creamy, lemon twist.

Oven-Browned Carrots

12 carrots, cut diagonally into 1¹/₂-inch slices
3 tablespoons olive oil
1¹/₄ teaspoons kosher salt
¹/₂ teaspoon freshly ground pepper
2 tablespoons minced fresh dill weed or flat-leaf parsley

Preheat the oven to 400 degrees. Combine the carrots, olive oil, salt and pepper in a large bowl and toss to coat. Arrange the carrots in a single layer on a large baking sheet. Roast for 20 minutes. Remove to a large bowl and add the dill weed, tossing to coat.

Serves 6 to 8

Roasted Cauliflower

1 head cauliflower, separated into florets
4 unpeeled garlic cloves
Bread crumbs
Olive oil
Kosher salt to taste

Preheat the oven to 400 degrees. Place the cauliflower and garlic on a baking sheet. Sprinkle with bread crumbs. Drizzle with olive oil and season with salt. Roast for 30 minutes or until the cauliflower is fork-tender and brown on the edges.

Serves 6

Roasted Fennel with Cherry Tomatoes

2 bulbs fennel with leafy tops
1 pint cherry tomatoes
1 cup pitted black olives
1 heaping tablespoon fresh thyme leaves
2 garlic cloves, peeled and
finely chopped

Sea salt and freshly ground pepper
to taste
1 cup white wine
2 tablespoons butter, cut into
small pieces

Preheat the oven to 425 degrees. Remove and finely chop the leafy fennel tops. Sprinkle the chopped fennel over the bottom of an 8×8-inch baking dish coated with nonstick cooking spray. Cut the fennel bulbs in half lengthwise and slice thinly. Place in the dish. Add the tomatoes, olives, thyme and garlic and season with salt and pepper. Add the wine and dot with the butter. Cover tightly with foil and bake on the middle oven rack for 20 minutes. Remove the foil and bake for 15 minutes longer.

Note: To make this a one-dish meal, top the vegetables with boneless skinless chicken breasts or white fish fillets (such as turbot or orange roughy) before baking.

Serves 4 to 6

Herb-Roasted Cherry Tomatoes

1 pound cherry tomatoes, cut into halves
1 to 2 garlic cloves, chopped
3 to 4 tablespoons olive oil
3 tablespoons fresh herbs, chopped
(such as parsley, basil, and thyme)
Kosher salt and freshly ground pepper to taste

Preheat the oven to 350 degrees. Toss the tomatoes and garlic with the olive oil and half the herbs in a large bowl. Season with salt and pepper to taste. Place the mixture in a shallow baking dish. Bake for 1 hour or until tender and slightly brown around the edges. Toss with the remaining herbs and serve.

Note: For a lovely salad, pour the hot tomatoes over fresh baby spinach to wilt. Top with crumbled blue cheese. Or do the same with arugula, freshly grated Parmesan, and a drizzle of balsamic vinegar.

Serves 2 to 4

Mushroom-Spinach Sauté

8 ounces button mushrooms, sliced
1 tablespoon olive oil
1 garlic clove, minced
2 (10-ounce) packages fresh spinach leaves
2 slices bacon, crisp-cooked and crumbled
1/4 cup (1 ounce) shredded or cubed mozzarella cheese
Salt and pepper to taste

Sauté the mushrooms in the olive oil in a large sauté pan or skillet over high heat until golden brown. Add the garlic and reduce the heat to medium. Add the spinach in batches and stir to combine. Cook each batch just until wilted and stir in more spinach. Turn off the heat when the last of the spinach has been added; stir. Sprinkle with the bacon and cheese and season with salt and pepper.

Serves 4

Oven-Roasted Corn on the Cob

Fresh, sweet corn still in the husks

Preheat the oven to 350 degrees. Remove the dried silks from the tops of the corncobs and any loose husks. Place the corn directly onto the oven racks. Roast for 25 minutes. Remove and cool for a few minutes. Remove the husks and silks and serve.

Note: Cooking corn this way retains its natural sweetness and
gives the corn a roasted texture and flavor.

Serves a variable amount

Fresh Corn Pudding

2 cups fresh corn kernels, or
2 (10-ounce) packages frozen corn
1/2 cup (1 stick) butter, melted
2 eggs
1 cup sour cream
1 cup (4 ounces) cubed or shredded

Monterey Jack cheese
1/2 cup cornmeal
1 (4-ounce) can diced green chiles
1 1/2 teaspoons salt
1 jalapeño chile, seeded and chopped
  (optional)

Preheat the oven to 350 degrees. Combine 1 cup of the corn, the butter and eggs in a blender or food processor and process until puréed. Combine the sour cream, cheese, cornmeal, green chiles, salt and jalapeño in a medium bowl and mix well. Stir in the puréed mixture until combined. Pour into a well-greased 2-quart baking dish. Bake, uncovered, for 50 to 60 minutes or until set and golden brown; a toothpick inserted in the center should come out clean. Serve with salsa, if desired.

Serves 6

FAMILY FAVORITES LIKE CORN PUDDING ARE A FAMILIAR menu item at many Marist events, from the monthly faculty appreciation luncheons to the grade-level socials hosted by the Marist Parents' Club each fall. For the past fifty years, the Parents' Club has been an invaluable support system for Marist students, parents, and staff, providing critical funding for program and facility enhancement, as well as operating valuable family services like the Campus Shop, Families in Action, and an annual used book sale. Ongoing special events sponsored by the Parents' Club, like Holiday Traditions and the Tour of Homes, welcome visitors from all over Atlanta to the Marist community.

Celery Root and Potato Gratin

1 teaspoon salt
1/2 teaspoon pepper
1/4 teaspoon nutmeg
3/4 cup thinly sliced shallots
2 (1-pound) celery roots, peeled,
halved and thinly sliced
2 pounds russet potatoes, peeled and thinly sliced
2 cups cream or heavy cream
1 cup chicken broth
2 cups (8 ounces) shredded fontina cheese

Preheat the oven to 400 degrees. Combine the salt, pepper and nutmeg in a small bowl. Sprinkle half the shallots on the bottom of a greased 10×15-inch baking dish. Top with half the celery root and half the potatoes. Sprinkle with half the salt mixture. Repeat the layers of shallots, celery root, potatoes and salt mixture. Combine the cream and broth in a small saucepan over medium heat. Bring to a simmer. Pour over the vegetable layers. Cover tightly with foil. Bake for 45 minutes. Remove the foil and press down firmly on the vegetable layers with the flat side of a spatula. Bake, uncovered, for 10 minutes or until the liquid has thickened. Top with the cheese and bake for 15 minutes longer. Let stand for 15 minutes before serving.

Serves 8 to 10

Overnight Mashed Potatoes

8 to 10 new potatoes, peeled
1 cup sour cream
8 ounces cream cheese, softened
6 tablespoons butter
1/3 cup chopped chives
3/4 cup (3 ounces) grated Parmesan cheese

Preheat the oven to 350 degrees. Cook the potatoes in a pot of boiling water until tender; drain well. Combine the sour cream and cream cheese in a large mixing bowl and beat well. Add the hot potatoes and beat until smooth. Add 2 tablespoons of the butter and the chives. Coat a 9×13-inch baking dish with 2 tablespoons of the butter and sprinkle with half of the Parmesan cheese. Spread the potatoes evenly over the cheese. Dot with the remaining 2 tablespoons butter and sprinkle with the remaining Parmesan cheese. The potatoes can be made 1 day ahead. Refrigerate covered. Bake, uncovered, for 25 minutes or until hot and bubbly.

Serves 10

Fanned New Potatoes

12 new potatoes
1/2 cup (1 stick) butter, melted
Kosher salt and pepper to taste
2 tablespoons chopped fresh rosemary, tarragon or dill weed
1/4 cup (1 ounce) freshly grated Parmesan cheese

Preheat the oven to 375 degrees. Cut each potato into thin slices, cutting almost to but not through the bottom. Place the potatoes in a 9×13-inch baking dish and spread the slices apart. Drizzle with half the butter and season with salt and pepper. Bake for 45 minutes. Drizzle with the remaining butter and sprinkle with the rosemary and cheese. Bake for 10 minutes longer or until tender and light brown.

Serves 6 to 8

Tri-Colored Potatoes

4 purple potatoes
3 Yukon gold potatoes
2 sweet potatoes
2 eggs
1 1/2 cups cream or heavy cream
1 cup (4 ounces) freshly grated
   Parmesan cheese

1 sprig fresh rosemary, leaves removed
   and finely chopped
Salt and pepper to taste
1 cup (4 ounces) freshly grated
   Parmesan cheese

Preheat the oven to 350 degrees. Cook each variety of potatoes separately in a saucepan of boiling water until tender. Cool and slice thinly. Whisk the eggs in a medium bowl. Whisk in the cream, 1 cup Parmesan cheese, the rosemary leaves, salt and pepper until combined. Spoon some of the cream mixture onto the bottom of a 9×13-inch baking dish coated with nonstick cooking spray. Alternate layers of the potatoes and the cream mixture until all the potatoes are used, ending with the cream mixture. Sprinkle with 1 cup Parmesan cheese. Bake for about 30 minutes or until the top is brown.

Note: A combination of Parmesan and shredded Gruyère cheese can also be used.

Serves 4

Roasted Sweet Potatoes

2 large sweet potatoes, peeled and
   cut into wedges
1 tablespoon olive oil

1/2 teaspoon salt
1/8 teaspoon ground allspice
1/8 teaspoon cayenne pepper

Preheat the oven to 500 degrees. Place the sweet potatoes in a large bowl and drizzle with the olive oil, tossing to coat. Stir together the salt, allspice and cayenne pepper in a small bowl. Sprinkle over the potatoes and toss to coat. Arrange the potatoes in a single layer on a baking sheet or shallow baking pan. Roast for 15 to 20 minutes or until tender and brown, turning after 10 minutes.

Serves 4

Spinach and Onion Gratin

1/4 cup (1/2 stick) unsalted butter
4 cups chopped Vidalia onions (about 2 large onions)
1/4 cup all-purpose flour
1/2 teaspoon nutmeg
2 cups 2% milk or whole milk
1 cup cream or heavy cream
5 (10-ounce) packages frozen chopped
spinach, thawed, drained and squeezed dry
1 cup (4 ounces) grated Parmesan cheese
1 tablespoon kosher salt
1/2 teaspoon pepper
1/2 cup shredded Gruyère cheese

Preheat the oven to 425 degrees. Melt the butter in a large skillet and add the onions. Sauté for 15 minutes or until golden brown. Stir in the flour and nutmeg until combined. Cook for 2 minutes, stirring occasionally. Add the milk and cream. Cook until thickened, stirring constantly. Add the spinach and half the Parmesan cheese and mix well. Season with the salt and pepper. Stir in the remaining Parmesan cheese and the Gruyère cheese. Pour into a greased 9×13-inch baking dish, spreading evenly. Bake for 20 to 25 minutes or until hot and bubbly.

Serves 8

Buttered Pecan Butternut Squash

1 large butternut squash
(about 2 pounds), halved, seeded,
peeled and cubed
2 tablespoons extra-virgin olive oil
1 tablespoon chopped fresh rosemary or
thyme leaves

Kosher salt to taste
Freshly ground pepper to taste
1 tablespoon unsalted butter
1/4 teaspoon freshly grated nutmeg
1 cup pecans, coarsely chopped
Additional freshly grated nutmeg

Preheat the oven to 400 degrees. Place the squash cubes in a large bowl and drizzle with the olive oil. Sprinkle with the rosemary, salt and pepper. Arrange the squash in a single layer on a large rimmed baking sheet or shallow baking pan. Roast for 45 minutes or until fork-tender and brown, stirring occasionally. Remove the squash to a serving bowl. Heat the butter and 1/4 teaspoon nutmeg in a small saucepan over medium-low heat until the foam subsides. Add the pecans and toast for about 4 minutes or until the butter and pecans are brown. Pour over the squash and stir lightly to coat. Season with salt and pepper and sprinkle with additional nutmeg.

Serves 4

Golden Curried Couscous

2 1/4 cups low-sodium chicken broth
3/4 cup raisins (optional)
6 tablespoons lemon juice
3 tablespoons finely chopped
crystallized ginger
1 tablespoon margarine
3/4 teaspoon curry powder

1 1/2 cups couscous
1/2 cup thinly sliced celery
1/3 cup thinly sliced green onions
1/4 cup chopped fresh cilantro
1/4 cup coarsely chopped pistachios
(optional)

Bring the broth to a boil in a saucepan over high heat. Stir in the raisins, lemon juice, ginger, margarine, curry powder and couscous. Cover the pan and remove from the heat. Let stand for 5 to 10 minutes or until the liquid is absorbed. Stir with a fork. Stir in the celery, green onions and cilantro just before serving. Sprinkle with the pistachios. Serve warm or at room temperature.

Serves 6

Wild Rice Pilaf

1 tablespoon butter
1 shallot, chopped
1 cup wild rice, rinsed
2 cups chicken broth
Juice of 1 lemon

1 to 2 tablespoons lemon zest
Salt and pepper to taste
1/2 cup chopped pecans, toasted
3 tablespoons chopped green onion
3 tablespoons chopped fresh parsley

Melt the butter in a saucepan over medium-high heat. Add the shallot and sauté until translucent. Add the rice and cook for 1 minute, stirring constantly.

Add the broth, lemon juice, lemon zest, salt and pepper and mix well. Bring to a boil over high heat. Reduce the heat and simmer, covered, for 30 to 45 minutes or until the rice is puffed and tender. Remove from the heat. Add the pecans, green onion and parsley; toss to combine.

Serves 4 to 6

Sesame Rice Cakes

3 cups cooked jasmine rice, cooled to
room temperature
1 tablespoon sugar
1 tablespoon rice vinegar

1 teaspoon cornstarch
1 teaspoon kosher salt
2 teaspoons sesame seeds
2 tablespoons (or more) vegetable oil

Combine the rice, sugar, vinegar, cornstarch and salt in a bowl and mix well. Spoon and press some of the rice mixture into a 1/4-cup measuring cup coated with nonstick cooking spray. Tap the cake onto a baking parchment paper-lined baking sheet. Repeat to shape cakes from the remaining rice mixture. Press 1/4 teaspoon sesame seeds gently onto the top of each rice cake. Heat 2 tablespoons oil in a skillet over medium-high heat. Add the rice cakes, seed side down, and sauté for 5 minutes on each side until golden brown, adding additional oil if needed. Serve immediately or keep warm in 200-degree oven.

*Note: Pair the Sesame Rice Cakes with Tuna with Wasabi Butter (page 81)
and Orange Cucumber Relish (page 37).*

Serves 8

Brunch & Breads

Warm and wonderful

selections to make a special morning

the tastiest time of the day.

Baked Orange Pecan French Toast

French Toast
4 eggs
2/3 cup orange juice
1/3 cup milk
1/4 cup sugar
1/2 teaspoon vanilla extract
1/4 teaspoon nutmeg
8 (1/2-inch) slices Italian or French bread
1/4 cup (1/2 stick) butter or margarine
1/2 cup chopped pecans

Orange Syrup
1/2 cup (1 stick) butter
1/2 cup sugar
1 cup orange juice

For the French toast, whisk the eggs in a medium bowl. Whisk in the orange juice, milk, sugar, vanilla and nutmeg until blended. Arrange the bread slices in a single layer in a large tray or shallow baking dish. Pour the egg mixture over the bread. Refrigerate, covered, for at least 2 hours. Preheat the oven to 350 degrees. Melt the butter in a 10×15-inch baking pan in the oven. Arrange the bread slices in the butter. Bake for 20 minutes. Sprinkle with the pecans and bake for 10 minutes longer. Serve with the orange syrup.

For the syrup, combine the butter, sugar and orange juice in a saucepan over low heat. Cook until the butter melts and the sugar dissolves, stirring constantly. Do not boil. Cool for 10 minutes. Pour into a serving dish and serve warm.

Serves 4

Holiday Morning French Toast

1 cup packed brown sugar
1 tablespoon ground cinnamon
3 Granny Smith apples, peeled
   and thinly sliced
1/2 cup dried cranberries
1/2 cup (1 stick) butter, melted

1 loaf French bread, cut into
   1-inch slices
6 eggs
1 1/2 cups milk
2 tablespoons ground cinnamon
1 tablespoon vanilla extract

Combine the brown sugar and 1 tablespoon cinnamon in a 9×13-inch baking dish. Stir in the apples and dried cranberries until coated. Spread the apple mixture evenly over the bottom of the dish. Drizzle with the melted butter. Arrange the bread slices on top, cutting to fit and covering the apples completely. Whisk the eggs in a large bowl. Whisk in the milk, 2 tablespoons cinnamon and the vanilla. Pour the mixture evenly over the bread. Refrigerate, covered, for 4 to 24 hours. Preheat the oven to 375 degrees. Bake, covered with foil, for 40 minutes. Remove the foil and bake for 5 minutes longer. Remove from the oven and let stand for 5 minutes. Cut into 8 squares and serve with warm maple syrup.

Serves 8

Tuscan Egg Bake

1 1/2 pound loaf rosemary
   foccacia bread, cubed
8 eggs
3 1/4 cups low-fat milk
1/4 cup sour cream
1/4 cup oil-pack sun-dried tomatoes,
   drained and chopped

1 garlic clove, minced
4 to 6 ounces prosciutto
12 ounces mozzarella cheese,
   thinly sliced
1/2 cup (2 ounces) freshly grated
   Parmesan cheese

Preheat the oven to 350 degrees. Arrange the bread cubes on a baking sheet. Bake for 10 minutes or until toasted.

Whisk the eggs, milk and sour cream in a bowl until blended. Stir in the tomatoes, garlic and bread cubes. Let soak for 5 minutes. Pour half the mixture into a greased 9×11-inch glass baking dish. Top with the prosciutto and mozzarella cheese. Pour the remaining egg mixture over the top. Chill, covered, in the refrigerator for 8 hours to overnight.

Bake, uncovered, for 20 minutes. Top with the Parmesan cheese. Bake for 20 minutes longer.

Serves 8 to 10

Pain Perdu with Mixed Berry Compote

Pain Perdu
2 eggs
1 cup sugar
1 tablespoon cornstarch
1 cup milk
$1/2$ teaspoon freshly grated nutmeg
1 loaf day-old French bread, cut into $3/4$-inch slices
Butter for frying

Mixed Berry Compote
2 teaspoons butter
$1/2$ cup sugar
2 tablespoons orange juice
Grated zest of 1 orange
3 pints assorted fresh berries

For the Pain Perdu, whisk the eggs in a large bowl. Whisk in the sugar and cornstarch until dissolved. Whisk in the milk and nutmeg. Add the bread slices and soak until the liquid is absorbed. Melt a small amount of butter in a large skillet over medium heat. Add the bread slices, a few at a time, and cook until golden brown on both sides, turning once. Remove to a pan and keep warm in the oven. Repeat frying the remaining bread slices, adding butter as needed.

For the compote, melt the butter in a medium saucepan over medium heat. Add the sugar, orange juice and orange zest and mix well. Cook until the sugar dissolves. Stir in the berries gently and cook over low heat just until the fruit is heated through. Keep the fruit intact. Serve immediately over the Pain Perdu.

Note: If using strawberries in the compote, half them before adding.

Serves 6

Huckleberry Hotcake

1/2 cup (1 stick) butter, softened
1 cup granulated sugar
1 egg
2 cups all-purpose flour
2 teaspoons baking powder
1/4 teaspoon salt
3/4 cup milk
1 teaspoon vanilla extract
1 to 1 1/2 cups huckleberries
Additional all-purpose flour for coating
Confectioners' sugar

Preheat the oven to 350 degrees. Cream the butter and granulated sugar in a large mixing bowl until light and fluffy. Beat in the egg. Stir together 2 cups flour, the baking powder and salt. Add the milk and flour mixture alternately to the sugar mixture, beating after each addition. Stir in the vanilla. Toss the berries gently with additional flour in a large bowl to coat lightly. Stir the berries into the batter. Pour into a greased 9×13-inch baking dish. Bake for 35 minutes or until a wooden pick inserted in the center comes out clean; do not overbake. Cool on a wire rack for 5 minutes before cutting into squares. Sprinkle with confectioners' sugar and serve warm.

Note: You may substitute blueberries, raspberries, and/or blackberries for the huckleberries.

Serves 10 to 12

A variety of seasonal fruits would work well with this recipe, making it the ideal brunch basic all year round. Experiment with these variations of this quick morning treat:

- Serve with a warm flavored syrup, such as strawberry or boysenberry.
- Replace the berries with your favorite seasonal fruit, such as peaches or apples.
- For a nutty flavor, substitute almond extract for a portion of the vanilla.
- Mix blackberries and blueberries into the batter and serve with a warm raspberry sauce.
- Drizzle with a light glaze instead of sprinkling with confectioners' sugar.

Puffy Apple Pancake

1/4 cup (1/2 stick) unsalted butter
4 Granny Smith apples or
Golden Delicious apples, peeled and
coarsely chopped
2 tablespoons light brown sugar
1/8 teaspoon ground cinnamon

4 eggs
1 cup milk
1 tablespoon granulated sugar
1/4 teaspoon salt
1/8 teaspoon ground cinnamon
2 tablespoons confectioners' sugar

Preheat the oven to 425 degrees. Melt the butter in a large ovenproof skillet or gratin pan over medium heat. Add the apples and brown sugar. Cook for about 20 minutes or until most of the liquid has evaporated and the apples have begun to caramelize, stirring frequently. Sprinkle with 1/8 teaspoon cinnamon. Combine the eggs, milk, granulated sugar, salt and 1/8 teaspoon cinnamon in a mixing bowl and beat well. Pour the egg mixture over the hot apples and place the skillet in the center of the oven. Bake for 20 minutes. Reduce the oven temperature to 350 degrees and bake for 15 minutes longer or until puffed and brown. Remove the pancake to a serving platter and sprinkle with the confectioners' sugar. Cut into wedges and serve immediately.

Serves 8

Almond Skillet Cake

*This tasty breakfast treat is a treasured recipe from a previous
Marist cookbook, A Touch of Atlanta.*

3/4 cup (1 1/2 sticks) butter, melted
1 1/2 cups sugar
2 eggs
1 1/2 cups all-purpose flour

1/2 teaspoon salt
1 teaspoon almond extract
1/2 cup slivered almonds
1/2 cup sugar

Preheat the oven to 350 degrees. Cream the butter and 1 1/2 cups sugar in a bowl until smooth. Beat in the eggs one at a time. Add the flour, salt and almond extract and mix well. Pour the batter into a greased iron skillet. Sprinkle with the slivered almonds and 1/2 cup sugar. Bake for 30 to 40 minutes. Let cool briefly and remove from the pan.

*Variation: This skillet cake is also delicious with a raspberry topping. Prepare and
bake the cake as described above, omitting the almond sugar topping. Remove from the oven
and let cool for a few minutes. Spread with raspberry jam and sprinkle with slivered almonds.
Return to the oven and bake for 10 minutes longer.*

Serves 8

Apple Raisin Bread Pudding

4 eggs	1 large Granny Smith apple,
1 cup sugar	peeled and diced
2 cups milk	2/3 cup raisins
3 tablespoons unsalted	7 slices white bread, crusts removed and
butter, melted	bread cubed (about 3 1/2 cups)
1/4 teaspoon ground cinnamon	Additional ground cinnamon
1/8 teaspoon salt	Vanilla Sauce

Preheat the oven to 350 degrees. Whisk the eggs in a large bowl. Add the sugar, milk, butter, 1/4 teaspoon cinnamon and salt and whisk until blended. Fold in the apple, raisins and bread cubes. Pour into a buttered 7×11-inch baking dish. Bake for 30 minutes. Sprinkle with additional cinnamon. Bake for 35 minutes longer or until the top is golden brown and the center is set. Spoon the pudding into serving dishes and top with Vanilla Sauce (below).

*Note: May be served as a dessert. It is wonderful with vanilla
ice cream or freshly whipped cream.*

Serves 6 to 8

Vanilla Sauce

2 cups cream or heavy cream	1 tablespoon vanilla extract
1/2 cup sugar	1/4 teaspoon salt
4 egg yolks	2 scoops vanilla ice cream
1 tablespoon all-purpose flour	

Bring the cream and sugar to a boil in a 2-quart saucepan, stirring constantly. Remove from the heat immediately. Beat the egg yolks, flour, vanilla and salt in a mixing bowl until smooth. Stir in a small amount of the hot cream mixture. Add the egg mixture to the remaining hot cream mixture and mix well. Cook until just beginning to thicken, stirring constantly; do not overcook. Remove from the heat and add the ice cream, stirring until melted. Strain the mixture into a small bowl or pitcher. Serve with the Apple Raisin Bread Pudding (above).

Serves 6 to 8

Cranberry Walnut Coffee Cake

¹/₂ cup (1 stick) butter, softened
1 cup sugar
2 eggs
1 teaspoon almond extract
2 cups all-purpose flour
1 teaspoon baking powder
1 teaspoon baking soda
¹/₂ teaspoon salt
1 cup nonfat plain yogurt
¹/₄ cup chopped walnuts
1 cup whole cranberry sauce
¹/₄ cup chopped walnuts

Preheat the oven to 350 degrees. Cream the butter and sugar in a large mixing bowl until light and fluffy. Beat in the eggs and almond extract. Stir together the flour, baking powder, baking soda and salt. Add half the flour mixture to the sugar mixture and mix well. Stir in the yogurt. Add the remaining flour mixture and ¹/₄ cup walnuts and mix well. Spread half the batter into a greased and floured 10-inch tube pan. Top with half the cranberries, and then the remaining batter, spreading evenly. Top with the remaining cranberries and ¹/₄ cup walnuts. Bake for 50 to 55 minutes or until a wooden pick inserted in the center comes out clean. Cool in the pan for 10 minutes. Invert onto a serving plate. Cut into wedges to serve. Serve warm.

Serves 12

Stuffed Strawberries

12 ounces cream cheese, softened
3 tablespoons confectioners' sugar
Grated zest of 1 lemon
1 teaspoon vanilla extract
24 large strawberries
Toasted sliced almonds for garnish

Beat the cream cheese in a mixing bowl until fluffy. Add the confectioners' sugar, lemon zest and vanilla and mix well. Trim the bottoms of the strawberries so that they stand upright. Scoop out the stems and centers of the strawberries with a melon baller. Pipe the cream cheese mixture into the centers of the strawberries. Garnish with almonds. Arrange the strawberries on a serving platter.

Serves 8

Fresh Melons with Ginger Syrup

1 1/2 cups sugar
1 1/2 cups water
1 (3-inch) piece fresh ginger,
peeled and sliced lengthwise
Assorted fresh seasonal melons, cubed
Fresh mint leaves, julienned

Heat the sugar and water in a saucepan over low heat, stirring until the sugar is dissolved. Add the ginger and bring to a boil. Reduce the heat and simmer, partially covered, for 15 minutes. Strain and cool the syrup. Place the melons in serving bowls. Drizzle with the syrup and sprinkle with mint.

Serves 6 to 8

Artichoke and Ham Strata

3 English muffins, split and quartered
1 tablespoon margarine, melted
1 cup chopped cooked ham
1/2 cup (2 ounces) grated Romano cheese
or Parmesan cheese
2 tablespoons chopped fresh chives
1 (14-ounce) can artichoke hearts,
drained and chopped

3 garlic cloves, minced
3 eggs
3 egg whites
1 (12-ounce) can evaporated fat-free
milk
1/8 teaspoon nutmeg

Arrange the muffin quarters crust side down in an 8×8-inch baking dish coated with nonstick cooking spray. Drizzle with the margarine. Top evenly with the ham, cheese, chives, artichokes and garlic. Whisk the eggs, egg whites, evaporated milk and nutmeg in a bowl until blended. Pour over the layers. Refrigerate, covered, for 8 hours or overnight. Preheat the oven to 375 degrees. Bake the strata, uncovered, for 50 minutes or until set. Remove from the oven and let stand for 10 minutes before serving.

Serves 6

Santa Fe Eggs

Spicy Tomato Sauce
2 tablespoons butter
1 cup chopped onion
2 garlic cloves, minced
1/2 teaspoon oregano
2 cups diced fresh tomatoes, or
1 (14-ounce) can petite diced tomatoes
1/4 teaspoon chili powder
Salt and pepper to taste

Eggs
1/4 cup (1/2 stick) butter
2 large poblano chiles, seeded and diced
1/2 cup chopped green onions
1/2 cup chopped fresh cilantro
8 large eggs, beaten
1 cup (4 ounces) queso fresco or
feta cheese

For the sauce, melt the butter in a large skillet over medium heat. Sauté the onion, garlic and oregano until tender. Add the tomatoes and chili powder and mix well. Simmer for 5 minutes. Pour the mixture into a blender and process until smooth. Season with salt and pepper. Keep warm.

For the eggs, melt the butter in the skillet. Add the chiles and sauté until tender. Add the onions and 1/4 cup of the cilantro and mix well. Add the eggs and cheese, stirring to combine. Cook until the eggs are fluffy, stirring frequently.

Serve with the sauce and the remaining 1/4 cup cilantro.

Serves 8

Tomato and Basil Basted Eggs

2 eggs
2 tablespoons halved grape tomatoes
1 tablespoon basil pesto
Salt and pepper to taste
1 teaspoon Mediterranean tangerine oil or olive oil
1 tablespoon grated Parmigiano-Reggiano cheese
1 teaspoon chopped fresh basil leaves

Preheat the oven to 350 degrees. Break the eggs side by side into an individual baking dish or ramekin. Top with the tomatoes and pesto. Season with salt and pepper and drizzle with the tangerine oil. Bake for 10 to 15 minutes or until the edges are bubbly and the yolks are cooked to desired doneness. Remove from the oven and sprinkle with the cheese and basil. Serve hot with applewood-smoked bacon.

Note: Mediterranean tangerine oil can be found at specialty grocery stores or
online at www.bellacucina.com.

Serves 1

THESE TOMATO AND BASIL BASTED EGGS ARE THE delightfully simple inspiration of renowned chef Alisa Barry, Marist class of 1982 and the talented founder of Bella Cucina Artful Food. A familiar presence in specialty stores and fine groceries around the country, Barry's award-winning line of pestos, pastas, and preserves reflect her love of Italian culinary traditions. Barry graduated from Vanderbilt University in Tennessee, and after studying at Tante Marie's Cooking School in San Francisco, moved to the California wine country. There she perfected her skills, creating dishes for a market owned by the Sebastiani family. In 1993, Barry returned to her Atlanta roots and opened a small café in an antique gallery on Bennett Street. Customer demand for her high quality spreads, oils, and pestos mushroomed, quickly evolving into a separate business featuring more than fifty specialty products. Today her signature jars have become pantry staples for gourmet cooks and food aficionados around the country.

Eggs Florentine

1 tablespoon margarine
1/2 to 1 pound mushrooms, sliced
1 bunch scallions, sliced
1 cup (4 ounces) shredded sharp
Cheddar cheese
1 (10-ounce) package frozen chopped spinach,
cooked, drained and squeezed dry
1 pound bulk pork sausage, cooked and crumbled
12 eggs
1 pint cream or heavy cream
1 cup (4 ounces) shredded Swiss cheese

Preheat the oven to 350 degrees. Heat the butter in a large sauté pan over medium-high heat. Add the mushrooms and scallions and sauté for 5 minutes or until the mushrooms are golden brown; drain any excess liquid. Sprinkle the Cheddar cheese evenly over the bottom of a lightly greased 9×13-inch baking dish. Top evenly with the spinach, and then the sausage. Spoon the mushroom mixture evenly over the top. Whisk the eggs in a large bowl until frothy. Whisk in the cream. Pour the egg mixture over the layers. Sprinkle the Swiss cheese over the top. Bake, loosely covered with foil, for 40 to 45 minutes or until set. Let stand for 10 minutes before serving.

Note: You may substitute 1 pound diced cooked ham for the sausage.

Serves 8 to 10

Easy Country Breakfast

6 eggs
3 cups milk
1 teaspoon dry mustard
1 teaspoon salt
10 slices white bread, crusts removed and bread cubed
2 cups (8 ounces) shredded sharp Cheddar cheese
4 to 6 ounces diced cooked ham
3 tablespoons finely chopped onion
2 tablespoons chopped fresh parsley

Preheat the oven to 325 degrees. Whisk the eggs in a large bowl until frothy. Whisk in the milk, dry mustard and salt until blended. Stir in the bread cubes, cheese, ham, onion and parsley until combined. Pour into a 7×11-inch baking dish. Bake for 1 hour or until the center is set. Let stand for 10 minutes before serving.

Serves 8

Try a Southwestern variation on this classic breakfast casserole.

Combine 1 garlic clove and 1/4 cup butter in a blender or food processor. Pulse the mixture until it reaches a paste consistency. Spread the garlic mixture on both sides of thickly sliced Italian bread (8 or 9 slices). Arrange the slices in a single layer in the bottom of a large baking dish. Use Pepper Jack cheese and chopped green onions instead of Cheddar cheese and regular onions. Serve with salsa on the side.

Frittata Primavera

6 garlic cloves, minced
2 red bell peppers, cut into thin strips
1 yellow bell pepper, cut into thin strips
1 large red onion, thinly sliced
1 tablespoon olive oil
Salt and pepper to taste
3 yellow squash, thinly sliced
3 zucchini, thinly sliced
1 tablespoon olive oil
1 pound mushrooms, sliced

1 tablespoon olive oil
6 jumbo eggs
1/4 cup cream or heavy cream
2 teaspoons sea salt
2 teaspoons freshly ground pepper
8 thick slices crusty sourdough
   bread, cubed
12 ounces cream cheese, cubed
12 ounces shredded Swiss cheese

Preheat the oven to 325 degrees. Sauté the garlic, bell peppers and onion in 1 tablespoon olive oil in a large skillet until tender. Season with salt and pepper to taste. Remove to paper towels to drain. Sauté the squash and zucchini in 1 tablespoon olive oil in the skillet until tender. Season with salt and pepper to taste. Remove to paper towels to drain. Sauté the mushrooms in 1 tablespoon olive oil in the skillet until tender. Season with salt and pepper to taste. Remove to paper towels to drain. Whisk the eggs in a large bowl until frothy. Whisk in the cream. Season with sea salt and 2 teaspoons pepper.

Stir the sautéed vegetables, half the bread cubes, the cream cheese and Swiss cheese into the egg mixture and mix well. Press the remaining bread cubes onto the bottom of a lightly greased 10-inch springform pan and place on a baking sheet. Pour the vegetable mixture into the pan. Bake for 1 hour or until set, covering with foil after 45 minutes to prevent overbrowning. Remove to a wire rack and cool in the pan for 10 minutes. Place on a serving platter and remove the side of the pan. Can be served hot, warm or chilled.

Serves 8

Hash Brown Quiche

1/2 (32-ounce) package frozen hash
brown potatoes, thawed
1/3 cup margarine, melted
1 to 1 1/2 cups (4 to 6 ounces) shredded Cheddar cheese
1 to 1 1/2 cups (4 to 6 ounces) shredded Swiss cheese
1 to 1 1/2 cups diced cooked ham, Canadian bacon or sausage
1/2 cup finely chopped onion (optional)
3 eggs
3/4 cup milk

Preheat the oven to 350 degrees. Spoon the hash browns into a 9-inch pie plate and drizzle with the margarine. Press onto the bottom of the pie plate to form a crust. Bake for 20 minutes. Remove from the oven and top the crust with the Cheddar cheese, Swiss cheese, ham and onion. Whisk the eggs and milk together in a bowl until blended. Pour over the layers, covering completely. Bake for 30 to 35 minutes or until set and golden brown; a toothpick inserted into the center should come out clean. Do not overbake. Remove from the oven and let stand for 5 minutes. Cut into wedges to serve.

Note: Other varieties of cheese can be substituted for the Swiss cheese. You may
also use a 10-inch pie plate. Add an additional egg and 1/4 cup milk.

Serves 6 to 8

Crustless Crab Quiche

8 ounces mushrooms, sliced
4 green onions, chopped
2 tablespoons butter
4 eggs
1 cup small-curd cottage cheese
1 cup sour cream
1/2 cup (2 ounces) grated Parmesan cheese
1/4 cup all-purpose flour
1/4 teaspoon salt
4 drops hot pepper sauce
2 cups (8 ounces) shredded Monterey Jack cheese
6 ounces crab meat, drained and flaked

Preheat the oven to 350 degrees. Sauté the mushrooms and green onions in the butter in a large skillet over medium-high heat until tender, stirring frequently. Drain on paper towels. Process the eggs, cottage cheese, sour cream, Parmesan cheese, flour, salt and hot sauce in a blender or food processor until blended, stopping once to scrape down the side of the container. Pour the egg mixture into a large bowl. Stir in the sautéed mushrooms, Monterey Jack cheese and crab meat. Pour into a greased 10-inch quiche dish or other shallow baking dish. Bake for 45 minutes or until set and light brown. Remove from the oven to a wire rack and let stand for 15 minutes before serving.

Serves 6 to 8

Stacked Smoked Salmon Pancakes

Pancakes
2/3 cup all-purpose flour
1/4 cup cornmeal
2 egg yolks
2/3 cup milk
1/2 cup diced red bell pepper
3 tablespoons chopped fresh cilantro
1/2 teaspoon red pepper flakes
Salt and pepper to taste
2 egg whites, at room temperature
1 tablespoon unsalted butter, melted

Smoked Salmon Topping
4 ounces cream cheese, softened
3 tablespoons sour cream
5 ounces smoked salmon, cut into
   40 to 46 strips
40 to 46 fresh cilantro sprigs
   for garnish

For the pancakes, combine the flour, cornmeal, egg yolks, milk, bell pepper, cilantro, red pepper flakes, salt and pepper in a medium bowl and mix well. Beat the egg whites in a small mixing bowl until stiff peaks form. Fold the egg whites into the batter. Heat a large nonstick skillet over medium heat and brush with the butter. Drop tablespoonfuls of the batter onto the skillet to form 1 1/4-inch pancakes. Cook for about 1 minute or until bubbles appear on the surface and the underside is golden brown. Turn and cook the other side until golden brown. Repeat the process using all of the batter.

For the topping, beat the cream cheese with the sour cream in a small bowl until fluffy. Pipe or spoon 1 teaspoon of the cream cheese mixture onto each pancake. Top with a twisted salmon strip and garnish with a cilantro leaf.

Makes 40 to 46 bite-size appetizers

Sweet Potato Bread

3 cups sugar	1 teaspoon nutmeg
4 eggs	1 1/2 cups mashed cooked sweet potatoes
1 cup vegetable oil	3 cups self-rising flour
1 teaspoon ground cinnamon	2/3 cup water or orange juice

Preheat the oven to 350 degrees. Combine the sugar, eggs, oil, cinnamon and nutmeg in a large mixing bowl and beat until smooth and blended. Add the sweet potatoes, flour and water and mix well. Pour into two lightly greased and floured 4×8-inch loaf pans. Bake for 45 to 60 minutes or until a wooden pick inserted in the centers comes out clean. Remove from the oven to a wire rack and cool in the pan for 5 minutes. Invert the loaves onto the rack and cool completely. Slice and serve.

Note: This bread freezes well and is delicious toasted.

Makes 2 loaves

Simply Delicious Rolls

1/2 cup (1 stick) butter, softened	1 cup sour cream
1/2 cup (1 stick) margarine, softened,	2 cups self-rising flour

Preheat the oven to 400 degrees. Cream the butter and margarine in a large mixing bowl until fluffy. Stir in the sour cream. Add the flour and mix well. Drop by rounded teaspoonfuls into miniature muffin pan cups lightly coated with nonstick baking spray. Bake for 10 to 15 minutes or until very light brown. Do not overbake.

Makes 12 to 18 rolls

Onion Foccacia

1 envelope dry yeast
1/4 cup warm water
3 cups all-purpose flour
1 teaspoon salt
1 cup warm water
1 teaspoon olive oil
2 onions, thinly sliced
1/2 cup olive oil
Salt to taste

Dissolve the yeast in 1/4 cup water in a small bowl. Combine the flour and 1 teaspoon salt on a work surface. Make a well in the center. Add the dissolved yeast and rub the mixture between the palms of your hands to blend. Make another well in the dough. Add 1 cup water slowly. Mix the dough and gather into a ball. Place 1 teaspoon olive oil on the work surface and knead the dough until smooth. Place the dough in a large bowl and cover with a damp cloth. Let rise for about 1 1/2 hours or until doubled in bulk. Punch down the dough and roll out to a 12×16-inch rectangle about 1/4-inch thick. Place the dough on a greased 12×16-inch baking sheet. Press the onions into the dough, making dents with your fingers. Spoon 1/2 cup olive oil over the dough and distribute evenly. Sprinkle lightly with salt to taste. Let stand at room temperature for 30 minutes. Preheat the oven to 400 degrees. Bake on the middle rack of the oven for 25 minutes or until brown.

Note: A mixer with a dough hook can be used to make the dough.

Makes one 12×16-inch foccacia

Desserts

From effortless to sophisticated,

sweet to satisfying,

these desserts are the perfect

end to a memorable meal.

Chocolate-Filled Pear en Croûte

6 Anjou pears
1 cup (6 ounces) semisweet chocolate chips
1 (17-ounce package) frozen puff pastry, thawed
1 egg
1 tablespoon water
2/3 cup (4 ounces) semisweet chocolate chips
3 tablespoons unsalted butter
1 (12-ounce) jar caramel sauce or raspberry sauce, warmed
Mint leaves, raspberries or strawberries for garnish

Peel the pears, leaving the stems intact. Cut off the tops of the pears just above the thickest part and reserve. Scoop out the cores using a melon baller, being careful not to cut through the sides or bottoms of the pears. Fill the cavities evenly with 1 cup chocolate chips and replace the tops of the pears.

Roll out the pastry on a lightly floured surface to a 10×13-inch rectangle and cut each into 4 squares. Place a pear in the center of 6 pastry squares and bring the corners together to cover the pear completely, pinching the edges to seal and leaving the stems exposed. Use the remaining 2 pastry squares to cover the top part of the pears. Beat the egg with the water in a small bowl. Brush the egg mixture over the pastry-wrapped pears. The pears can be prepared up to 24 hours ahead; refrigerate, covered with plastic wrap.

Preheat the oven to 425 degrees. Place the pears on an ungreased baking sheet and bake for 15 minutes. Reduce the oven temperature 375 degrees and bake for 5 to 8 minutes longer or until the pastry is puffed and golden brown. Melt 2/3 cup chocolate chips in a double boiler or a small saucepan placed over boiling water, stirring until smooth. Remove from the heat and whisk in the butter until melted.

To serve, spoon the caramel sauce onto 6 individual serving plates and top with the pears. Drizzle with the chocolate glaze and garnish with mint leaves.

Serves 6

Orange Cream Crepes

Crepes
2 eggs
2 teaspoons sugar
$^1/_2$ teaspoon salt
$^1/_2$ cup all-purpose flour
$1^1/_3$ cups milk
2 tablespoons butter, melted

Filling
1 cup heavy whipping cream,
  well chilled
1 tablespoon confectioners' sugar
2 tablespoons Cointreau or other
  orange-flavored liqueur

Orange Sauce
$^1/_4$ cup ($^1/_2$ stick) butter, softened
1 cup sugar
Grated zest of 1 orange
$^1/_2$ cup orange juice
1 egg, well beaten

For the crepes, beat the eggs in a small mixing bowl until frothy. Beat in the sugar and salt until blended. Beat in the flour and milk alternately until blended. Stir in the butter. The batter will be thin. Lightly grease a small sauté pan or skillet and heat over low heat until hot. Stir the batter and ladle 3 to 4 tablespoons into the pan, tilting to coat the bottom evenly, forming a 5- to 6-inch crepe. Cook the crepe for 1 minute or until set and light brown. Loosen the edge of the crepe; turn over and cook the other side until set. Repeat with the remaining batter. Stack the crepes between sheets of waxed paper or baking parchment paper and cool completely.

For the filling, combine the cream and confectioners' sugar in a chilled deep mixing bowl and beat until stiff peaks form. Fold in the Cointreau. Place a heaping tablespoonful of the filling in the center of each crepe and fold the edges into the center to make a square, completely enclosing the cream filling. Freeze between sheets of waxed paper in an airtight container.

For the sauce, combine the butter, sugar, orange zest, orange juice and egg in a small saucepan over medium heat. Cook until the mixture comes to boil, stirring constantly.

To serve, pour the orange sauce into a large skillet or chafing dish and heat to simmering. Add the frozen crepes, 2 or 3 at a time, and heat for 2 to 4 minutes, spooning the sauce over constantly. Serve warm.

Note: These crepes can be made weeks ahead. The flavor is reminiscent of a "creamsicle."

Serves 12

Triple Berry Cobbler

2 pounds strawberries
3 pints blueberries
2 pints raspberries
1 cup sugar
4 to 5 tablespoons cornstarch

2 tablespoons lemon juice
3/4 cup (1 1/2 sticks) butter, softened
2/3 cup almond paste
2/3 cup sugar
2 cups all-purpose flour

Preheat the oven to 400 degrees. Combine the berries, 1 cup sugar, cornstarch and lemon juice in a large bowl and stir gently until combined. Pour the berry mixture into a 9×13-inch baking dish. Place the butter, almond paste, 2/3 cup sugar and the flour in a food processor and process until crumbly. Sprinkle the crumb mixture evenly over the berry mixture. Bake for 45 minutes. Remove from the oven and cool for 5 minutes before serving. Serve warm with ice cream.

Serves 8

Raspberry Truffle

3/4 cup (1 1/2 sticks) unsalted butter
4 ounces unsweetened chocolate, chopped
3 eggs
2 cups granulated sugar
1/3 cup seedless raspberry jam
3 tablespoons black raspberry liqueur, such as Chambord, or other berry-flavored liqueur

1 cup all-purpose flour
1/2 teaspoon salt
1 cup (6 ounces) semisweet chocolate chips
Confectioners' sugar

Preheat the oven to 350 degrees. Melt the butter and unsweetened chocolate in a double boiler or in a saucepan placed over boiling water, stirring until smooth. Whisk in the eggs, granulated sugar, jam and liqueur until blended. Stir in the flour, salt and chocolate chips just until combined. Pour the chocolate mixture into a 9-inch springform pan coated with nonstick cooking spray. Bake for 45 minutes. Remove to a wire rack to cool completely. Remove the side of the pan. Sprinkle with confectioners' sugar and cut into wedges to serve.

Serves 8 to 10

Snowflake Pudding with Crimson Sauce

Pudding
1 cup sugar
1 envelope unflavored gelatin
1/2 teaspoon salt
1 1/4 cups milk

2 cups heavy whipping cream,
  well chilled
1 teaspoon vanilla extract
1 (3 1/2-ounce) can flaked coconut

Crimson Sauce
1 (10-ounce) package frozen raspberries, thawed
1 1/2 teaspoons cornstarch
1/2 cup red currant jelly

For the pudding, combine the sugar, gelatin and salt in a saucepan and mix well. Add the milk and cook over medium heat until the gelatin and sugar dissolve, stirring constantly. Pour into a large bowl and chill, covered, in the refrigerator for 30 to 45 minutes or until partially set. Pour the cream into a chilled large mixing bowl and beat until stiff peaks form. Remove the gelatin mixture from the refrigerator and stir in the vanilla. Fold in the coconut, and then the whipped cream. Pour into a 1 1/2-quart mold or 8 individual dishes or wine glasses. Chill in the refrigerator for 4 to 6 hours or until set. Unmold the pudding onto a serving platter. Serve with the sauce.

For the sauce, combine the raspberries, cornstarch and jelly in a small saucepan over medium heat. Bring to a boil. Cook until the mixture is thickened and translucent, stirring constantly. Strain the mixture through a sieve into a bowl, pressing with a spoon to crush the berries. Chill in the refrigerator before serving.

Note: If using individual dishes or wine glasses, there is no need to unmold.

Serves 8

Mango Lime Mousse

Raspberry Sauce
1 (10-ounce) package frozen
   raspberries, thawed
1/2 cup sugar
1/4 cup black raspberry liqueur,
   such as Chambord

Mousse
1 envelope unflavored gelatin
1/2 cup fresh lime juice
2 ripe mangoes
1/2 cup cream or heavy cream

For the sauce, combine the raspberries, sugar and liqueur in a blender and process until puréed. Strain the mixture through a sieve into a bowl. Chill in the refrigerator for 2 hours or until ready to serve.

For the mousse, sprinkle the gelatin over the lime juice in a small saucepan and let stand for 10 minutes. Peel the mangoes and cut the flesh from the seeds. Combine the mangoes and the cream in a blender and process until puréed. Heat the lime juice over low heat to dissolve the gelatin. Stir in the mango mixture and mix well. Pour into a 3-cup mold or spoon into individual martini glasses. Chill in the refrigerator for 3 hours or until set. Pour the sauce over the mousse before serving.

Serves 4 to 6

Summer Fruit with Praline Fondue

Summer Fruit
1/2 cup crème fraîche
1 1/2 teaspoons dark brown sugar
1/2 cup chopped pecans, toasted
Assorted fresh fruit, such as grapes,
   berries, sweet cherries,
   plum wedges and peach wedges

Praline Fondue
6 tablespoons unsalted butter
1 cup packed dark brown sugar
2 tablespoons water
2 1/2 tablespoons dark rum
1 teaspoon vanilla extract

For the fruit, combine the crème fraîche and 1 1/2 teaspoons brown sugar in a medium bowl and mix well. Pour into a small serving bowl. Place the pecans in a small serving bowl. Arrange the bowls of crème fraîche and pecans on a serving platter or tray and surround with the fruit.

For the fondue, melt the butter in a medium nonstick skillet over medium heat. Increase the heat to medium-high and add the brown sugar and water. Cook for 1 minute, stirring constantly. Stir in the rum and vanilla. Pour the fondue into a serving bowl.

To serve, dip the fruit in the fondue then into the pecans and crème fraîche.

Makes 1 1/2 cups fondue

Cream Puffs with Chocolate Sauce

Puffs
1 cup water
1/2 cup (1 stick) margarine
1/4 teaspoon salt
1 cup all-purpose flour
3 eggs

Filling
1 pint heavy whipping cream,
   well chilled
1/2 cup confectioners' sugar
1/2 teaspoon vanilla extract

Chocolate Sauce
4 ounces semisweet baking chocolate
1/4 cup water
1/4 cup sugar
2 tablespoons butter

For the puffs, preheat the oven to 400 degrees. Combine the water, margarine and salt in a medium saucepan and bring to a full rolling boil. Remove from the heat and add the flour all at once, stirring vigorously until the mixture forms a ball. Remove the dough to a large mixing bowl and beat in the eggs 1 at a time. Drop the dough by teaspoonfuls onto a greased or baking parchment paper-lined baking sheet. Bake for 10 minutes. Reduce the oven temperature to 325 degrees and bake for 25 minutes longer or until golden brown. Remove to a wire rack and cool completely. The puffs can be frozen at this point in sealable freezer bags. Thaw at room temperature and heat in a warm oven for 2 to 3 minutes before filling. Slice off and reserve the tops of the puffs. Remove the soft dough from the insides of the puffs.

For the filling, combine the cream, confectioners' sugar and vanilla in a chilled large mixing bowl and beat until peaks begin to form. Spoon the whipped cream into the puffs and replace the tops.

For the sauce, stir together the chocolate and water in a small saucepan over low heat. Cook until the chocolate has melted and the mixture is smooth, stirring constantly. Add the sugar and cook until blended, stirring constantly. Stir in the butter until smooth. Spoon the warm sauce over the filled puffs.

Makes 16 to 20 medium puffs

Caramel Pastry Puff

2 (14-ounce) cans sweetened
condensed milk

1 1/2 (17-ounce) packages frozen puff
pastry, thawed (3 sheets)

Preheat the oven to 425 degrees. Pour each can of sweetened condensed milk into an 8- or 9-inch pie plate and cover with foil. Place the pie plates in larger shallow pans. Fill the larger pans with hot water. Bake for 1 to 1 1/2 hours or until thick and light caramel-colored. Scrape the caramel into a large bowl and beat until smooth.

Reduce the oven temperature to 400 degrees. Roll out the pastry sheets on a lightly floured surface to 12×16-inch rectangles. Place on baking sheets and bake for 15 to 20 minutes or until golden brown. Cool; cut each pastry sheet in half.

Place 1 pastry sheet on a large serving tray and spread with a layer of the caramel. Repeat layering the pastry and caramel. Press down on the pastry stack to crush, and then top with the remaining caramel. Sprinkle any pastry crumbs on top. The pastry can be made ahead. Cut into squares to serve.

Note: The sweetened condensed milk can also be caramelized in the microwave oven. Pour 1 can sweetened condensed milk into a 2-quart glass measure. Microwave on 1/2 power (Medium) for 4 minutes, stirring vigorously after 2 minutes. Reduce to 1/3 power (Low) and microwave for 12 to 16 minutes or until thick and light caramel-colored, stirring vigorously every 2 minutes until smooth. Repeat with the second can of sweetened condensed milk.

Serves 12 to 15

Fresh Fruit Pastry Puff

1/2 (17-ounce) package frozen
puff pastry, thawed (1 sheet)
2 cups strawberries, blueberries
and raspberries

1 to 2 tablespoons honey
1 cup whipped cream

Preheat the oven to 400 degrees. Roll out the pastry sheet on a lightly floured surface and cut into 6 squares. Place on a baking sheet and bake for 15 minutes or until golden brown; cool. Combine the berries and honey in a bowl, stirring to crush the fruit slightly to release the juices. Let stand for 10 minutes. Place the pastry squares on 6 individual serving plates. Top evenly with the fruit and whipped cream.

Serves 6

Southern Praline Cheesecake

Crust
1¼ cups graham cracker crumbs
3 tablespoons sugar
⅓ cup butter, melted

Filling
1⅓ cups chopped pecans
3 tablespoons butter, melted
24 ounces cream cheese, softened
1 cup packed dark brown sugar

2 tablespoons all-purpose flour
3 extra-large eggs
1 teaspoon vanilla extract

Praline Topping
1½ teaspoons granulated sugar
¼ cup packed dark brown sugar
2 tablespoons cream or heavy cream
1 tablespoon butter
½ teaspoon vanilla extract

For the crust, preheat the oven to 350 degrees. Combine the graham cracker crumbs and sugar in a small bowl and mix well. Add the butter and stir until combined. Press the mixture onto the bottom of a 9-inch springform pan. Bake for 8 minutes.

For the filling, preheat the oven to 350 degrees. Combine the pecans and butter in a small bowl, stirring until coated. Spread evenly on a baking sheet and toast for 3 to 5 minutes or until golden brown, stirring once; cool. Reduce the oven temperature to 325 degrees. Combine the cream cheese, brown sugar and flour in a large mixing bowl and beat until light and fluffy. Beat in the eggs 1 at a time. Stir in the vanilla. Reserve ¼ cup of the pecans for the topping. Stir the remaining pecans into the filling. Pour the filling over the crust and bake for 1 hour. Turn the oven off and let the cheesecake stand in the oven for 30 minutes. Remove to a wire rack and loosen the side of the pan. Cool completely before removing the side of the pan.

For the topping, combine the granulated sugar, brown sugar, cream and butter in a small saucepan. Bring to a boil. Cook until the sugar dissolves, stirring constantly. Reduce the heat to low and cook to 225 degrees on a candy thermometer, or just under the soft-ball stage. Remove from the heat immediately and cool slightly. Stir in the vanilla until creamy. Sprinkle the reserved pecans over the cheesecake and drizzle with the praline topping. Chill in the refrigerator for at least 8 hours. Place on a serving platter. Cut into wedges.

Serves 10 to 12

Sour Cream Cheesecake

Crust
1¹/2 cups chocolate cookie crumbs
¹/4 cup (¹/2 stick) butter, melted

Filling
24 ounces cream cheese, softened
1 cup sugar
4 eggs
2 tablespoons vanilla extract
2 cups sour cream
¹/4 to ¹/3 cup Irish cream liqueur
Whipped cream or fresh fruit for garnish

For the crust, combine the cookie crumbs and butter in a bowl and mix well. Press onto the bottom and up the side of a 10-inch springform pan. Chill in the refrigerator while preparing the filling.

For the filling, preheat the oven to 500 degrees. Beat the cream cheese in a large mixing bowl until light and fluffy. Beat in the sugar gradually until smooth. Beat in the eggs 1 at a time. Stir in the vanilla. Fold in the sour cream and liqueur. Pour the filling over the crust and bake for 8 minutes. Reduce the oven temperature to 225 degrees and bake for 50 minutes longer. Turn off the oven and leave the door ajar. Let the cheesecake stand in the oven for 20 minutes. Remove to a wire rack and cool completely. Loosen the side of the pan. Chill in the refrigerator for 8 hours. Remove the side of the pan and place the cheesecake on a serving platter. Cut into wedges. Garnish each serving with whipped cream or fresh fruit.

Serves 10 to 12

Decadent Mousse Cake with Espresso Cream

Cake
2 cups (4 sticks) butter
16 ounces semisweet chocolate, chopped
1 cup sugar
1 cup water
1 teaspoon instant coffee granules (optional)
8 eggs, lightly beaten

Espresso Cream
1½ cups heavy whipping cream, well chilled
1 tablespoon ground dark roast coffee
½ cup sugar

For the cake, preheat the oven to 350 degrees. Combine the butter, chocolate, sugar, water and coffee granules in a heavy 3-quart saucepan over low heat. Cook until the chocolate is melted and the mixture is smooth, stirring constantly. Remove from the heat. Stir a small amount of the hot mixture into the eggs. Stir the eggs into the chocolate mixture until blended. Pour into a greased 9-inch springform pan. Bake for 45 to 50 minutes or until a wooden pick inserted in the center comes out clean. Remove to a wire rack to cool completely. Remove the side of the pan. Chill, covered with plastic wrap, in the refrigerator for at least 4 hours. Place on a serving platter and cut into wedges. Serve with the espresso cream.

For the espresso cream, combine the cream and coffee in a chilled large mixing bowl and beat until foamy. Add the sugar gradually, beating until stiff peaks form.

Serves 16

Delicious and slightly decadent, this cake is easy to prepare, elegant to serve, and worth every calorie.

- Add an impressive finishing touch once the cake has completely cooled by sprinkling confectioners' sugar through a paper doily to create a lacy effect on the top.
- Once cake has been chilled, garnish with fanned strawberries. Fan a strawberry by thinly slicing about ⅔ of the way to the stem being careful to not cut all the way through. Leave the stems on. Gently separate slices to fan out. Arrange strawberries around the perimeter of the cake, leaving two or three strawberries to place on a dollop of whipped cream in the center.
- Can also be served with warmed Crimson Sauce (page 145) and freshly whipped cream.

Dulce de Leche Ice Cream Cake

Crust
1 cup graham cracker crumbs
1 tablespoon sugar
1/4 cup (1/2 stick) butter, melted

Filling
3 pints dulce de leche ice cream
2 pints strawberry sorbet

Topping
2 pounds fresh strawberries, sliced
2 tablespoons sugar
Caramel sauce or dulce de leche sauce

For the crust, preheat the oven to 350 degrees. Combine the graham cracker crumbs, sugar and butter in a bowl and mix well. Press onto the bottom of a 10-inch springform pan. Bake for about 8 minutes or until golden brown. Cool completely.

For the filling, slightly soften 1 pint of the ice cream and spread over the crust. Freeze for about 1 hour or until firm. Slightly soften 1 pint of the sorbet and spread over the ice cream. Freeze for about 30 minutes or until firm. Repeat layering with the remaining ice cream and sorbet. Freeze, covered, for at least 3 hours or up to 1 week.

To assemble, combine the strawberries and sugar in a large bowl and stir gently. Let stand for 30 minutes. Loosen the edge of the cake from the pan and remove the side of the pan. Cut the cake into wedges. Drizzle caramel sauce onto individual serving plates and top each with a cake wedge. Spoon the strawberries over the top.

Serves 16

Citrus Cream Cake with Lime Glaze

Cake
3¼ cups cake flour
¼ teaspoon baking soda
¼ teaspoon salt
1 cup plus 2 tablespoons unsalted butter, softened
8 ounces cream cheese, softened
3 cups sugar
6 eggs, at room temperature
3 tablespoons fresh lime juice, at room temperature
1 teaspoon vanilla extract
2 teaspoons grated lime zest

Glaze
¼ cup fresh lime juice
¾ cup granulated sugar
Confectioners' sugar

For the cake, position the oven rack in the lower third of the oven and preheat the oven to 325 degrees. Sift the flour, baking soda and salt over a sheet of waxed paper. Combine the butter and cream cheese in a large mixing bowl and beat on medium speed for 30 seconds or until smooth and creamy. Add the sugar gradually, beating for about 5 minutes or until light and fluffy, scraping down the side of the bowl frequently. Increase the speed to medium-high and beat in the eggs 1 at a time until blended. Beat in the lime juice and vanilla. Reduce the speed to low and add the flour mixture in 3 additions, beating just until combined and scraping the side of the bowl occasionally. Fold in the lime zest.

Spoon the batter into a greased and floured rose- or cathedral-shape tube cake pan or 10-cup bundt pan, spreading so that the sides are higher than the center. Bake for about 1½ hours or until golden brown and a wooden pick inserted in the center comes out clean. Remove to a wire rack and cool in the pan for 15 minutes. Set the wire rack over a sheet of waxed paper. Invert the pan onto the rack and lift off the pan.

For the glaze, whisk the lime juice and granulated sugar in a small bowl until blended. Brush the warm cake with the glaze. Cool completely. Dust with confectioners' sugar before serving.

*Note: It is important that all the cake ingredients be at
room temperature before mixing.*

Serves 16

Heavenly Chocolate Cake

Cake

1 (18-ounce) package devil's
food cake mix
1 (4-ounce) package chocolate
instant pudding mix
1/2 cup canola oil
3/4 cup orange juice
1/2 cup water
4 eggs
1/3 to 1/2 cup miniature semisweet
chocolate chips

Butter Icing

1/2 cup (1 stick) unsalted butter, softened
1 pound confectioners' sugar
1/8 teaspoon salt
11/2 teaspoons vanilla extract
2 to 3 tablespoons milk or cream

For the cake, preheat the oven to 350 degrees. Line the bottoms of two 8- or 9-inch cake pans with waxed paper or baking parchment paper and grease generously. Combine the cake mix, pudding mix, canola oil, orange juice, water and eggs in a large mixing bowl and beat at medium speed for 2 minutes or until blended. Fold in the chocolate chips. Divide the batter equally between the prepared pans. Bake for 30 to 45 minutes or until wooden picks inserted in the centers come out clean. Remove to a wire rack and cool in the pans for 10 minutes. Invert the cakes onto the rack and cool completely.

For the icing, beat the butter in a large mixing bowl until creamy. Add half the sugar, beating until smooth. Add the remaining sugar and beat until smooth. Beat in the salt and vanilla until blended. Beat in the milk 1 tablespoon at a time until the icing is smooth and spreadable. Spread the icing between the layers and over the top and side of the cake.

Serves 10 to 12

Raspberry Almond Layer Cake

Raspberry Sauce
3¹/₂ pints raspberries
¹/₄ cup sugar
1 tablespoon Grand Marnier or
other orange-flavored liqueur

Cake
5 tablespoons milk
¹/₂ teaspoon lemon juice
¹/₂ cup (1 stick) butter, softened
¹/₂ cup sugar
4 egg yolks

1 cup cake flour
1 teaspoon baking powder
Dash of salt
4 egg whites, at room temperature
1 cup sugar
¹/₂ cup slivered almonds
1¹/₂ cups heavy whipping cream,
  well chilled
1 teaspoon Grand Marnier or other
  orange-flavored liqueur
1 pint raspberries
Additional whipped cream

For the sauce, combine the raspberries, sugar and liqueur in a blender and blend to a purée. Strain the sauce through a fine-mesh strainer to remove all the seeds. Chill, covered, in the refrigerator until ready to serve.

For the cake, preheat the oven to 300 degrees. Combine the milk and lemon juice in a small bowl and mix well. Let stand for 10 minutes to curdle. Cream the butter and sugar in a large mixing bowl until light and fluffy. Add the egg yolks and beat well. Sift together the flour, baking powder and salt over a sheet of waxed paper. Add the flour mixture alternately with the milk mixture to the batter, beginning and ending with the flour and mix well after each addition. Divide the batter equally between 2 greased and floured 9-inch cake pans.

Beat the egg whites in a deep mixing bowl until foamy. Beat in the sugar gradually until stiff peaks form. Spread the egg white mixture evenly over the cake batter. Sprinkle with the almonds. Bake for 30 to 35 minutes or until the cakes test done. Remove to a wire rack and cool in the pans for 10 minutes. Remove from the pans to the rack and cool completely.

Place 1 cake layer almond side down on a serving plate. Combine the cream and liqueur in a chilled large mixing bowl and beat until stiff peaks form. Spread the whipped cream over the cake layer and top with the raspberries. Top with the second cake layer, almond side up. Serve with the raspberry sauce and additional whipped cream.

Serves 8 to 10

Terrific Traditional Pound Cake

1 cup (2 sticks) butter, softened
3 cups sugar
6 eggs, at room temperature
3 cups all-purpose flour

1 cup cream or heavy cream,
at room temperature
1 tablespoon vanilla extract

Cream the butter and sugar in a large mixing bowl for 10 minutes or until very light and fluffy. Beat in the eggs 1 at a time until blended. Add the flour and cream alternately, beating after each addition just until combined. Stir in the vanilla. Pour into a greased and floured 10-inch tube pan and place in the oven. Bake at 325 degrees for 1½ hours or until a wooden pick inserted in the center comes out clean. Remove to a wire rack and cool in the pan for 10 minutes. Remove the cake from the pan and cool completely.

Note: The oven is not preheated in this recipe.

Serves 10 to 12

Add a bit of flair to a favorite dessert!

- Mix 1 pint of diced strawberries, 1 mango, 1 plum, 1 nectarine, and 1 cup blueberries with ¼ cup sugar, zest of 1 lemon, juice of ½ lemon, and 2 tablespoons Sambuca liqueur; chill for at least 6 hours or overnight. Just before serving, add a diced banana and spoon over a slice of pound cake with a mint leaf for garnish.
- Top slices of pound cake with a berry medley of your choice. Add Grand Marnier sauce (see recipe on page 157) and fresh whipped cream.
- Toast slices of pound cake in the toaster or broiler, and top while warm with your favorite ice cream and hot fudge sauce.

Grand Marnier Sauce

2 egg yolks
1/4 cup sugar
2 tablespoons Grand Marnier
1/2 cup heavy whipping cream

Select a 1-quart heat-proof glass mixing bowl that will rest snugly on top of a slightly larger saucepan. Add about two inches of water to the saucepan and bring it to a boil over high heat. Reduce the heat to medium.

Place the egg yolks and sugar in the mixing bowl and beat vigorously with a wire whisk until smooth. Set the mixing bowl inside the saucepan, over but not in the water. Continue beating constantly and vigorously for 7 to 10 minutes or until the yolk mixture is thick and pale yellow. Remove the bowl from the saucepan and stir in the Grand Marnier.

Scrape the mixture into a chilled mixing bowl and place the bowl into the freezer until chilled; do not freeze. Place the cream into a mixing bowl and beat until stiff peaks form. Fold the whipped cream into the chilled Grand Marnier mixture. Serve with pound cake and fresh berries.

Serves 2

Key Lime Pie

1 (14-ounce) can sweetened
condensed milk
4 egg yolks
1/2 cup key lime juice

1 egg white, at room temperature
1 (9-inch) graham cracker crust
Freshly whipped cream and raspberries
for garnish

Preheat the oven to 350 degrees. Combine the sweetened condensed milk, egg yolks and lime juice in a large bowl and mix well. Beat the egg white in a small mixing bowl until stiff peaks form. Fold the egg white into the egg yolk mixture. Pour into the crust. Bake for 15 to 20 minutes or until set. Remove to a wire rack to cool. Chill in the refrigerator for 1 to 3 hours, or until firm. Garnish with freshly whipped cream and fresh raspberries.

Serves 6

Jamaican Fudge Tart

1¹/₂ refrigerator pie crusts, or pastry
for one 10-inch crust
¹/₄ cup (¹/₂ stick) butter, softened
³/₄ cup packed dark brown sugar
3 eggs
2 cups (12 ounces) semisweet chocolate chips
2¹/₂ teaspoons instant espresso coffee granules
Pinch of salt
2 teaspoons boiling water
2 teaspoons dark Jamaican rum
¹/₄ cup all-purpose flour
1 cup chopped pecans, toasted
1 to 2 cups pecan halves, toasted
1 egg
2 teaspoons cream or heavy cream

Preheat the oven to 400 degrees. Line the bottom of a 10-inch tart pan with 1 pie crust. Cut 1-inch strips from the remaining pie crust and line the side of the pan, pinching to seal and completely covering the bottom of the pan. Prick the bottom and side with a fork. Bake the crust for 11 minutes. Remove to a wire rack and cool; do not cover or refrigerate the crust. Reduce the oven temperature to 375 degrees. Cream the butter and brown sugar in a large mixing bowl until light and fluffy. Beat in 3 eggs 1 at a time, scraping down the side of the bowl occasionally. Melt the chocolate chips in a glass bowl coated with nonstick cooking spray in the microwave for 2 minutes on High. Stir until smooth. Add the chocolate to the butter mixture and mix well. Stir together the coffee granules, salt and water in a small bowl until the coffee and salt are dissolved. Stir in the rum. Stir the rum mixture into the chocolate mixture. Sprinkle the flour over the chocolate mixture and beat until smooth, scraping the side of the bowl once. Fold in the chopped pecans. Pour the filling into the crust. Decorate the top of the tart with the pecan halves. Beat 1 egg with the cream in a small bowl and brush over the pecans and the edge of the pastry. Bake for 25 minutes. Remove to a wire rack and cool slightly. Serve warm with coffee ice cream or cinnamon ice cream, if desired.

Serves 8 to 10

Mascarpone Peach Tart

Crust
1 1/2 cups all-purpose flour
3 tablespoons confectioners' sugar
1/4 teaspoon salt
1/2 cup (1 stick) unsalted butter,
chilled and cut into small pieces
3 1/2 tablespoons (about) ice water

Filling
1/4 cup sugar
3 tablespoons all-purpose flour
2 teaspoons grated lemon zest
6 ripe peaches, peeled, halved and cut
into 1/2-inch slices (about 4 cups)
2 tablespoons honey
2 tablespoons unsalted butter,
chilled and cut into small pieces
2 tablespoons peach preserves, melted

Mascarpone Cream
1 cup heavy whipping cream,
well chilled
6 tablespoons mascarpone cheese
2 tablespoons sugar
1/4 teaspoon vanilla extract

For the crust, combine the flour, confectioners' sugar and salt in a food processor and process until blended. Add the butter and pulse until the mixture is crumbly. Add the water, 1 tablespoon at a time, processing constantly until a dough forms. Gather the dough into a ball and flatten to a disk. Wrap in plastic wrap and chill in the refrigerator for 1 hour. Roll out the dough on a lightly floured surface to a 12-inch round. Place the crust in a 9-inch tart pan with a removable bottom. Press into the pan and trim, leaving a 1-inch edge of dough extending around the pan. Fold the trim into the pan and press into the side of the crust to form a double thickness. Press the inside edge of the crust to form an 1/8- to 1/4-inch rim above the edge of the pan. Prick the bottom of the crust with a fork. Chill in the refrigerator for 1 hour. Preheat the oven to 400 degrees. Bake for 25 minutes or until golden, piercing with a fork if bubbles appear during baking. The crust can be made 1 day ahead. Cool completely, wrap in plastic wrap and store at room temperature.

For the filling, preheat the oven to 400 degrees. Combine the sugar, flour and lemon zest in a large bowl. Add the peaches and stir gently to combine. Pour into the baked crust. Drizzle with the honey and dot with the butter. Bake for about 35 minutes or until the peaches are tender. Remove to a wire rack and brush the top of the tart with the preserves. Cool for 15 minutes before cutting. The tart can be made 6 hours ahead. Store at room temperature. Cut into wedges. Serve warm or at room temperature with the mascarpone cream.

For the mascarpone cream, combine the cream, mascarpone cheese, sugar and vanilla in a chilled deep mixing bowl and beat until stiff peaks form.

Serves 6

Summer Berry Tart

Crust
8 whole graham crackers, broken
1/4 cup packed light brown sugar
1/4 cup (1/2 stick) unsalted butter, melted

Filling
6 ounces cream cheese, softened
1/3 cup sugar
1/2 cup sour cream
2 teaspoons freshly squeezed lemon juice
1/2 teaspoon vanilla extract
1/2 pint raspberries or strawberries
1/4 cup seedless raspberry jam or strawberry jam

For the crust, preheat the oven to 375 degrees. Combine the graham crackers and sugar in a food processor and process until crumbly. Add the butter and process until evenly moistened. Press the crumb mixture onto the bottom of a 9-inch tart pan with removable bottom or springform pan. Bake for about 8 minutes or until firm to the touch. Remove to a wire rack to cool.

For the filling, combine the cream cheese and sugar in a medium mixing bowl and beat until smooth. Beat in the sour cream, lemon juice and vanilla. Pour the filling into the baked crust, spreading evenly. Chill, covered, in the refrigerator for at least 4 hours or up to 1 day.

To serve, arrange the raspberries over the filling. Stir the jam to pourable consistency and drizzle over the berries. Serve immediately or chill in the refrigerator for up to 3 hours.

Serves 8

Chocolate Macadamia Biscotti

1/2 cup (1 stick) unsalted butter, softened
1 1/4 cups sugar
2 eggs
1 1/2 teaspoons vanilla extract
2 cups all-purpose flour
1/3 cup baking cocoa
1 1/2 teaspoons baking powder
1/2 teaspoon salt
1 cup chopped macadamia nuts
2/3 cup semisweet chocolate chips, or chopped bittersweet or
semisweet baking chocolate

Preheat the oven to 350 degrees. Cream the butter and sugar in a large mixing bowl until light and fluffy. Beat in the eggs and vanilla until blended. Sift together the flour, baking cocoa, baking powder and salt over a sheet of waxed paper and add gradually to the butter mixture, mixing until a dough forms. Stir in the macadamia nuts and chocolate chips. Place the dough on a lightly floured surface and knead until smooth. Divide the dough in half and shape each half into a 3×10-inch log. Place the logs 3 inches apart on an ungreased baking sheet. Bake for 25 to 30 minutes or until a wooden pick inserted in the center comes out clean. Let stand until cool. Reduce the oven temperature to 325 degrees. Cut each log diagonally into eighteen 1/2-inch slices. Place the slices on the baking sheet and bake for 10 minutes. Turn the slices over and bake for 10 minutes longer. Remove to a wire rack and cool.

Makes 36 biscotti

Menu Ideas

Perfect for a special occasion,

a cozy family meal,

or a pleasant evening with friends —

enjoy these menus

every season of the year.

Terrific Tailgates

Early Fall Favorites

OLIVE TAPENADE   page 21

BLUE CHEESE PARSLEY DIP   page 23

TAILGATE SANDWICH   page 60

JALAPENO BASIL SLAW   page 40

ASSORTED COOKIES

Wonderful Warm-Ups

BLACK-EYED PEA SALSA WITH CHIPS   page 25

RED PEPPER DIP WITH FRESH VEGETABLES   page 24

WHITE LIGHTNING CHILI   page 55

BACON-WRAPPED BREADSTICKS   page 55

BROWNIES

Simply Scrumptious

ORANGE CUCUMBER RELISH   page 37

TUNA WITH WASABI BUTTER   page 81

SESAME RICE CAKES   page 119

GREEN BEAN BUNDLES   page 108

MANGO LIME MOUSSE   page 146

Dinner Party with Panache

Holiday Feast

Traditional Sunday Supper

Spring Brunch

Graduation Buffet

Summer Evening Picnic

Cookbook Committee

Pam Betz

Peggy Carlson

Sue Casserly

Kathy Cote

Kathleen de Groot

Ann Durot

Denise Fisher

Mary Harvey

Cindy Hunt

Nancy Jackson

Jane Keller

Terry Lamberski

Mary Anne Lanier

Angie Lewis

Barbara McGraw

Sally McNulty

Christine Nort

Peggy Schuster

Recipe Testers

Cherie Abernethy
Debbie Andrews
Pam Arena
Mapy Ashton
Cathi Athaide
Carla Bailey
Melanie Barton
Brenda Beadles
Pam Betz
Silvia Bowen
Libby Bowling
Ruthie Brown
Dorothy Burns
Rita Campbell
Peggy Carlson
Sue Casserly
Iris Chang
Sharon Coleman
Tammy Connell
Gail Craine
Mary Celine Crawford
Lori Crunk
Ruthy Cunningham
Angel Deedy
Claudia DeLoach
Laura Fawcett
Nancy Fayard
Liz Fetter
Kathrine Garcia
Marcel Gilli
Susanne Gleaton

Susanne Greenwood
Jane Gutschenritter
Mary Harvey
Holly Hayes
Kathy Herald
Helen Hodack
Julie Hodack
Debbie Horigan
Cindy Hunt
Jane Keller
Jayne Kloster
Jo Ann Konencamp
John Lambis
Kathryn Lambis
Mary Anne Lanier
Angie Lewis
Roanne Locarnini
Denise Long
Mary Lynn Lowery
Jan Mackenzie
Bonnie Martin
Amy Mathes
Beth McGaw
Sally McNulty
Nancy Meyer
Sherry Morsches
Shelly Mulick
Fiona Nemetz
Christine Nort
Joanne Quinn
John Rhett

Toni Rhett
Susan Roche
Queenie Ross
Laurie Rummel
Bob Schack
Peggy Schack
Katie Schmitz
Susan Spann
Jim Stelljes
Beth Stevens
Tami Stout
Ellen Sullivan
Dolores Svensson
Nancy Vieira
Dana Whitledge
Tim Withrow
Kathy Wochele
Terry Wortham
Pam Zimmermann
Liz Zivalich

Recipe Contributors

Cherie Abernethy

Patrick Albrecht

Susan Anderson

Pam Arena

Cathi Athaide

Carla Bailey

Karlene Barger

Alisa Barry

Carol Barry

Virginia Bart

Brenda Beadles

Lee Berg

Pam Betz

Phyllis Betz

Carol Boucher

Silvia Bowen

Libby Bowling

Mary Brown

Ruthie Brown

Dorothy Burns

Polly Callison

Rita Campbell

Jennifer Cannady

Peggy Carlson

Sue Casserly

Lois Catherman

Alan Chadwick

Iris Chang

Grace Cleary

Kathy Cleveland

Kathy Coghlan

Susan Cole

Brian Collier

Kathryn W. Collier

Anne Connolly

Peggy Connors

Marie S. Corrigan

Kathy Cote

Gail Craine

Mary Celine Crawford

Lori Crunk

Nancy Darden

Jaime Davenport

Angel Deedy

Lisa DeGrace

Kathleen de Groot

Claudia DeLoach

Kimberly Duckworth

Mimi Dukes

Anne Durot

Fr. Richmond Egan, S.M.

Kay Embry

Sharon Callison Falconer

Laura Fawcett

Eenee Ferrano

Liz Fetter

Denise Fisher

Mary Fletcher

Chrissie Fontaine

Kathy Fowler

Jeannae Geist

Terry Gilchrist

Marcel Gilli

Mary Gleason

Susanne Gleaton

Susanne Greenwood

Judy Guebert

Gretchen Gunning

Denise Gurn-Callaway

Jane Gutschenritter

Christine S. Hampton

Gail Harmeier

Mary Ann Hart

Mary Neal Harvey

Holly Hayes

Mary Hayes

Barbara Heath

Jeanne Heekin

Harry Henning

Kathy Herald

Loretta E. Hicks

Helen Hodack

Julie Hodack

Ann Hoedeman

Cindy Hunt

Cynthia Isaf

Nancy Jackson

Lynne Jones

Laura Kasperzak

Ashlie Kerr

Gerry King

Grace E. King

JoAnn Konenkamp

Recipe Contributors

Fr. Joel Konzen, S.M.
Trevor Kunk
Terry Lamberski
Todd James Lane
Lynn Lanier
Mary Ann Lanier
Susie LeGates
Corinne Leibrandt
Camille Leverett
Angie Lewis
Laura Lewis
Betty Long
Denise Long
Melissa Longosz
Mary Love
Mary Lynn Lowery
Margo Luckovich
Maria Ludi
Joanne Lyons
Diane Mahaffey
Arthur Markwell
Julie Marshall
Lois Matarrese
Amy Mathes
Denise McEnaney
Barbara McGraw
Lisa McNearney
Sally McNulty
Tammy Meredith
Nancy Meyer
Sandy Miller

Gordon Morrow
Sherry Morsches
Shelly Mulick
Fiona Nemetz
Norma Nicholson
Christine Nort
Dan O'Brien
Theresa O'Donnell
Amy O'Donoghue
Jenna Olsen
Elizabeth Opraseuth
Gina C. Parnaby
Annie Peterle
Jean Price
Joanne Quinn
Lib Quirk
Carol Raney
Joan Rearick
Sher Reene
Cheryl Rhodes
Queenie Ross
Barbara Rossie
Cecelia Palma Ruiz
Ann Rushing
Suzy Chmiel Russell
Celeste Sawyer
Katie Schmitz
Peggy Schuster
Amanda Scoles
Douglas Seanor
Marcia Shurley

Elizabeth Sikes
Tanya C. Sommers
Susan Spann
Elise Spina
Carolyn Sprinkle
Mimi Stamper
Malinda Steed
Jim Stelljes
Tamara Stout
Annie Sullivan
Ellen Sullivan
Magy Tadros
Mary Tippins
Cindy Tynes
Kate VanVolkenberg
Nancy Vieira
Claire Walls
Ray Wathen
Gail Weekley
Katie Weston
Gena White
Dana Whitledge
Mary Jo Winer
Teresa Winer
Pam Withrow
Marie Wood
Lindsay Wortham
Liz Zivalich

Index

Index

Index

Index

Index